Looking Forward to
MORE
Monday
Mornings

To 1-B

Looking Forward to
MORE
Monday
Mornings

How to Drive Your Colleagues Happy!

★ ★ ★

DIANE HODGES

A JOINT PUBLICATION

NATIONAL ASSOCIATION OF ELEMENTARY SCHOOL PRINCIPALS
Serving All Elementary and Middle Level Principals

CORWIN PRESS
A SAGE Publications Company
Thousand Oaks, CA 91320

For information:

Corwin Press
A Sage Publications Company
2455 Teller Road
Thousand Oaks, California 91320
www.corwinpress.com

Sage Publications Ltd.
1 Oliver's Yard
55 City Road
London EC1Y 1SP
United Kingdom

Sage Publications India Pvt. Ltd.
B-42, Panchsheel Enclave
Post Box 4109
New Delhi 110 017 India

Printed in the United States of America.

Library of Congress Cataloging-in-Publication Data

Hodges, Diane.
Looking forward to more Monday mornings : how to drive your colleagues happy! / Diane Hodges.
    p. cm.
Includes index.
ISBN 978-1-4129-4218-8 (cloth)—ISBN 978-1-4129-4219-5 (pbk.) 1. Teaching—Awards.
2. Teachers—Job satisfaction. 3. Incentive awards. I. Title.

LB2842.22.M645 2007
371.1—dc22

2006034597

This book is printed on acid-free paper.

08   09   10   11   10 9 8 7 6 5 4 3 2

Acquisitions Editor:	Elizabeth Brenkus
Editorial Assistant:	Desirée Enayati
Production Editor:	Jennifer Reese
Typesetter:	C&M Digitals (P) Ltd.
Cover Designer:	Rose Storey
Graphic Designer:	Lisa Miller
Illustrator:	John Speeter
Interior Design:	Jaye Pratt

Table of Contents

III. Celebrating with Coworkers

About the Author

Diane Hodges is Managing Director of
Threshold Group, an educational consulting
firm in San Diego. After 30+ years as an
educator, she is sharing her insights through
books and international speaking events. Her
wit and humor have delighted audiences and
readers everywhere. She served as a executive director of career and technical education, director of instruction, director of
human resources, secondary principal,
university instructor, and elementary and middle school counselor.
She earned her doctorate from Michigan State University, has
received twelve national and state leadership awards, and is the
author of seven books.

About the Illustrator

John Speeter began drawing cartoons and
illustrations while attending Michigan State
University. His drawings have been published
nationally in books, newsletters, and periodi-
cals, as well as on the Web. John's creativity
extends beyond his artistic abilities; he is also
an accomplished musician who plays numerous string instruments and performs in a
bluegrass group that appears throughout the
Midwest. Additionally, he is a health care
operations executive in Michigan.

Acknowledgments —

Thank you to the many schools, named and unnamed, who contributed ideas to this book. It is because of their sharing that this book is a reality.

I especially want to thank and acknowledge Debra Macklin and the Quincy Community Schools. I have never met Deb, but she was a HUGE contributor to this effort. Jennings Elementary School incorporates many fun, motivating activities into their school year, and she shared them with all of us in this book.

A special thanks goes to John Speeter, the creator of all the wonderful cartoon illustrations. Aside from being multitalented, he is truly a best friend. I count on him in so many ways and, as always, he came through with me on this effort.

I had a great team of people who worked together . . . Laurie Gibson of Word Association who did the editing . . . Jaye Pratt of Book Works who did the text design and graphics . . . and, of course, so many people at Corwin Press had a hand in this effort, especially Elizabeth Brenkus, Acquisitions Editor, and Desirée Enayati, Editorial Assistant.

And thanks goes to my family . . . I cherish them so much.

—D.

Introduction —

When *Looking Forward to Monday Morning* was first published, I felt I'd shared every possible morale-boosting idea in my brain, and never entertained the possibility of writing a sequel. During my book tours across the United States and Canada, numerous educators told me, "In my school we are doing _____." They had amazing ideas to share with other educators. What a wonderful profession we are in—people share so freely! I felt much like a troubadour, carrying ideas from district to district, state to state, and country to country. This book is a compilation of those incredible ideas, suggestions that can help you and your colleagues look forward to Monday morning!

It's Monday Morning!

Do you start the workweek on Monday—or MOANday—mornings? (It's also been referred to as "Monday MOURNings.") There's a scientific explanation behind the Monday morning blues: over the weekend, our bodies build up a sleep deficit of at least one hour. So when Monday morning rolls around, we want to stay snuggled in bed, not get up and face the workweek routine.

Monday has long had a negative stigma surrounding it. The former Soviet space agency banned Monday for any launches after four space ships blew up on Monday launches. It is a well-known perception that you should never purchase a car that was manufactured on Monday. People who call in sick after the weekend are known to have the "Monday flu," and more people die of heart attacks on Monday than any other day of the week. The term "Monday morning quarterback" refers to rearview thinking rather than strategic planning. There is an old wives' tale that "Marry on Monday, always poor."

One of my friends works for a very well-known computer company. Each Monday morning his supervisor meets with the staff. These meetings are called "Monday Morning Beatings" by those who attend. They hear about the mistakes they made the previous week and are criticized for them. Not surprisingly, they dread Monday mornings.

But Mondays are one-seventh of our lives, so we may as well learn to make the most of them—even enjoy and look forward to them! In this book, you'll find dozens of ideas to help change your attitude about Mondays from dread to delight. Here's one, just to help get you on your way:

Organizations always seem to plan special events on Fridays, but Friday is the start of the weekend (and often payday), so people are inclined to feel eager about it anyway. Why not schedule fun events on Monday, so people will look forward to and celebrate that day as well? It can only help boost morale, enjoyment, and creativity in the workplace. Give it a try—there's really nothing to lose!

Fun in the Workplace

A common fear (misconception) about having fun in the workplace is that it's a "waste of time." But taking time away from the job can actually increase productivity. Many people suffer from the disease of being too serious. But it is possible to be professional and still have fun—really.

I taught at the university level for 15 years as an adjunct professor. One semester I shared a media center with another extension class held at the same time. About half way through the semester, the Dean called me to her office. The professor with whom I shared the media center had complained about me. She told the Dean that my class laughed too much, so my students were obviously not learning. In reality, there was a great deal of learning going on, but we were *enjoying* the journey as well.

Another way of infusing fun into an organization can be seen in the following example. A year or two ago, I received a call from a woman who ordered a copy of my book and wanted to pick it up in person. When she arrived she explained that her husband was the *Minister of Fun* at one of the area universities. *Minister of Fun?* I'd never heard of that job title before. What a great occupation that must be! I asked her what he did, and she explained that his job was to create an environment that was rich, fun, rewarding, and creative. Since then I've found that there are many similar job titles, including *Director of WOW, Minister of Joy, Manager of Mirth, Ambassador of Playfulness, Vice President of Solutions, Vice President of Social Responsibility.* I wonder how much these jobs pay; I think I want to apply!

The presentations I give (based on my book) are sometimes attended by people who aren't fun. There's a part in the session when the group is asked to stand and sing "I'm the Principal," "I'm the Counselor," or "I'm the Assistant," depending on the audience. This often results in the mass migration of male principals who are very uncomfortable with that activity. It makes me wonder about the atmosphere in their schools.

After one presentation, two teachers stayed and asked a lot of questions. They lamented about how they had a new principal and the climate had changed from joyous to glum. One of the teachers said, "We are just going to have appoint ourselves as the *Ambassadors of Fun* for our school." As they walked out, I heard one of them say, "Today is the first time I've laughed in two weeks." If you find your-self in this situation, it's up to you and your colleagues to make your workplace fun—in spite of your principal.

And even if you're not a fun person, you can contribute to a fun work environment just by letting others implement fun activities. Schedule the first "Fun Committee" meeting, elect a chairperson, and watch it grow from there. People *crave* the chance to have fun.

Recognition and Appreciation

In addition to a fun environment, recognition and appreciation are crucial for educators. With this framework, it became apparent to me that a teacher reaches the top of the career ladder the first day he or she steps into the classroom.

People who spend their lives teaching will not receive promotions, bonuses, matched 401(k) contributions, profit

Teacher

Intern

Aide

sharing—motivators in other career fields. What motivates us is recognition and appreciation from colleagues, administrators, community members, parents, and students for a job well done.

Ask yourself if you typically acknowledge good performance. When you go to a theater and watch the singers, dancers, actors, what do you do at the end of the show? Do you say, "That's their job. They are paid to perform and entertain me," and then just leave the theater? Or do you applaud, shout, whistle, even stand up, for a job well done?

Now think about your school or office. How do you acknowledge a colleague when that person does really good work? Do you say, "The staff members are getting paid to do a good job so they don't need praise"? Remember, there's a huge difference between compensation (money) and recognition.

Staff members need to be appreciated for their efforts; they need to be thanked and recognized when they do a good job. People want to work where their skills are appreciated; the best people will stay in those environments.

It's important that the recognition be both timely and sincere. Sometimes the recognition will be informal, other times, formal. It may be one-to-one or it may be public. It's important to know what type of recognition each person wants and needs.

I always gave my boss a Christmas gift; each year I sent him a cheese assortment. That was a generic gift, appropriate for a female employee to send to a male supervisor. After 10 years, he casually mentioned in a staff meeting, " . . . you know, I really hate cheese." Gulp! I'd been giving him something he *hated*— for an entire decade! Did he appreciate that I sent him a gift? Probably. But I gave him something he didn't like. When you receive your paycheck, you're grateful to be paid for your work. But if the paycheck was in Euros, you wouldn't be as happy because even though you received a paycheck, it was in a currency you couldn't use. Keep the recipient in mind so you can give the person the appropriate kind of recognition.

This reminds me of a story about someone who was to be given an award for perfect attendance. This person was very private, and the recognition was going to be very public. The award was to be given at a big staff gathering; recipients were going to be on stage in front of all the other employees. This was such an uncomfortable situation that the person with perfect attendance actually called in sick that day—to avoid the public recognition! Think about the recipient; what would make that person happy?

Educators often hear that there just isn't money in the budget for recognition events, or that the Board would never allocate funds for these types of events. But the truth is simple: Recognition doesn't need to be "budgeted." What's really important is what happens when everyone is together. It doesn't have to be a gala, catered event—it can be a community potluck and still be meaningful. Some of the most effective forms of appreciation—saying thank you, giving someone a smile, a note, a hug, or a handshake—cost nothing. Just make sure they have the two essential elements: timeliness and sincerity.

And although everyone is worthy of receiving praise, sometimes people aren't comfortable giving it. During a break in one of my seminars on recognition and appreciation (the audience was a group of educators, many of whom were principals), a woman from another session asked how one of the participants was doing. I said he was doing great, but wondered why she asked. She explained that he was her principal and that the staff had taken up a collection to pay for his registration because they wanted him to develop the skills.

If you sometimes find it awkward to express appreciation, take heart—the pages of this book are brimming with ideas that can help you and your colleagues develop the ability to comfortably give recognition and appreciation.

A Final Note

Creating a rich, rewarding school workplace is everyone's job; we are all part of the "village" that it takes to raise (or educate) a child—and to contribute to future generations. In addition, we cannot help but thrive when working with motivated, enthusiastic colleagues; our own lives become richer as a result. Use the ideas in this book freely to invigorate yourself and "rev up" your coworkers so that everyone can benefit from the positive energy in your work environment. ***Drive your colleagues HAPPY!***

Section I

Recognition & Appreciation

There is more hunger for love and appreciation
in this world than for bread.
—Mother Teresa

Chapter 1
Recognizing Specific Behaviors

REWARDING GOOD BEHAVIOR

You often see trucks with "How's my driving? Call 555-5555" painted on the back. I saw a truck with a twist on that message: "How's my driving? **We reward safe driving.** Call 555-5555."

How's my driving?
We reward
safe driving.
Call 555-5555

> Celebrate what you want to see more of.
>
> —*Thomas J. Peters*

    The company made it very clear to anyone who was reading the sign that it valued safe driving; so much so that they rewarded those who practiced that behavior.

    What behaviors would you like to have rewarded in your school?

ATTENDANCE—STAFF AND PARENTS

Off-campus Lunch

Form the staff members into teams. The team with the best attendance for a specified length of time receives a coupon for a two-hour off-campus lunch. The administrators cover the classrooms while the winners are away.

Blue Jeans Pass

Each month, give staff members with the best attendance two passes that allow them to wear blue jeans to work. Make stickers for staff members to wear on Jeans Day that say, "I have Great Attendance and earned this Jeans Day."

Success Assemblies

At the end of each marking period staff members and students are recognized for perfect attendance as well as other successes.

Half Day Off

Encourage staff members to get parents to participate in events such as Parent Information Night and parent conferences. The teacher from each grade level with the highest percentage of parents attending the events receives a half day off. The administrators and counselors serve as substitutes in the classrooms. *(Chisholm Trail Elementary School, Sanger, TX)*

"My Time Off"

Parking Space Drawing

Put the names of staff members who have perfect attendance for the week in a container for a drawing. The person whose name is drawn gets the parking spot of his or her choice for the week. Hold the drawing at the weekly staff meeting or on Monday morning, and announce the winner during the daily announcements. Make a sign designating the winner's special parking spot.

CLASSROOM CLEANLINESS

Golden Dustpan Award

Each week (or month) the night custodian selects the cleanest classroom and the winner is announced on the P.A. system. The principal gives the award to a student from the winning room; the award is displayed in the classroom for a month.

PEER RECOGNITION

Above and Beyond Award

Give an award for staff members who go **A**bove and **B**eyond the **C**all of duty in service to colleagues. This helps focus attention on staff-to-staff relationships, and promotes inter-dependence, collaboration, and peer recognition. Using an "ABC" card, staff members nominate each other by describing how the nominee went above and beyond in order to help a colleague. Recognize the winners at staff meetings by reading the card aloud, presenting a personalized certificate suitable for framing, and awarding a congratulatory letter and gift certificate from an area restaurant or other suitable business. Make an "ABC" bulletin board and put it in a public location. Copy the narrative from the card and post it on the bulletin board, along with a picture of the honoree. *(Karyn Brownlee, Principal, Lee Elementary School, Coppell, TX)*

There is no letter I in TEAM

Acknowledgment Areas

Designate areas throughout the school as "peer recognition zones." For staff members it may be the copy room or staff lounge. Tape acknowledgements to the wall every week and include in the morning announcements when appropriate. After acknowledgements are removed from the wall, give them to the recipient (these make great portfolio items).

Variation: Create a "Thank You Board," where staff members can attach notes of thanks written on cutouts or Post-it Notes. At the end of the month, hold a drawing to select one of the notes on the board. The winner receives a monetary award. *(Crowell Independent School District, Crowell, TX)*

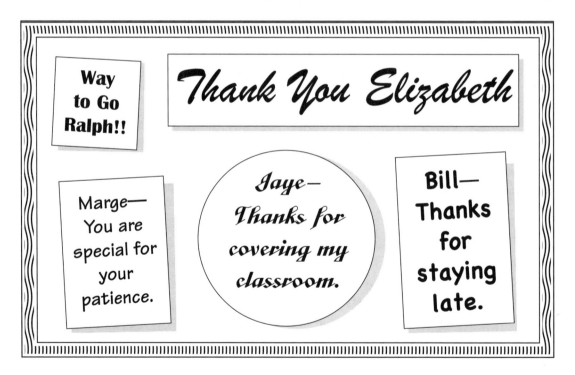

Magic Notes

Give "Magic Notes" to staff members who help their colleagues (e.g., covering an assigned duty for another). Submit them to the principal to read at the Monday morning assembly. Students can be rewarded in the same manner.

Treat Cart

At the start of the school year, ask staff members to list their favorite beverage and snack food. Keep this information in a file. Throughout the year, encourage staff members to nominate their peers to be awarded "a treat break." Select one staff member each week to receive treats, and include a note explaining why he or she was nominated.

Kindness Coins

At the start of the school year, give staff members a supply of gold medallion coins; these represent emotional currency of appreciation. Staff members then give the coins to their peers throughout the year as a way of expressing thanks.

Gratitude Bowl

The principal begins the activity by decorating a bowl with balloons and filling it with 10 candy bars. He or she takes the bowl to a staff member and thanks the person for doing something special. The staff member selects a candy bar and then takes the bowl to another person deserving of thanks. The bowl continues to be passed to others until all candy bars are gone.

If you can't say something nice, why not?

Recognition Postcards

During a staff meeting give each person a postcard to self-address. Collect the cards and distribute them again so that no one gets their own. Ask staff members to write a positive comment about the person whose name and address appears on the postcard and then sign it. Collect and mail the completed cards. Staff members will look forward to receiving their card of praise and recognition. And the staff lounge might be buzzing with the positive comments people have received in the mail.

Variation: Save the postcards and mail them out over the course of a month or periodically during the year. *(Phineas Davis Elementary School, York, PA)*

Back Scratchers

Give each staff member a piece of tagboard or large piece of construction paper with a string attached so it can be worn around the neck. Have them put the paper around their necks so that it rests on their back. Ask staff members to write what they appreciate about their colleagues on the papers. Post the sheets in each staff member's classroom or shrink them so they can be put in their portfolios.

Angel Award

Purchase an angel to use as a traveling award. At a staff meeting, give the award to a staff member who has done something significant behind the scenes for students or another staff member. The first week's recipient decides who the next recipient will be, and so on. *(Paw Paw High School, Paw Paw, MI)*

Extra Hand Award

Create a hand by using a see-through plastic glove (not one that is powdered, such as an examination glove). Fill the glove with popcorn or another type of treat and tie it off at the wrist. Draw fingernails with magic marker or nail polish. Attach a note such as, "The extra hand you gave certainly came in handy" or "Thanks for lending us a hand."

"I Care" Bear

Dress or decorate a stuffed bear in your school colors and attach a card and note such as the following:

> I'm your friendly "I Care" Bear, and I am here to remind you that someone cares. I can only stay with you for today, so pass me on to someone else. Before passing me on, PLEASE sign and date the back of my card. Have a "Beary" Good Day!

It's a great booster to receive the bear, see where it's been, and select the next recipient. *(Villa Rica Middle School, Temple, GA)*

"Beary" Special

Buy a small stuffed bear and attach a small spiral notepad to it. Laminate a sheet that says, "Let a staff member know something you like about him or her by writing a note in the notepad and putting the bear on his or her desk. Recipient: Pass the bear on to someone else within three days." *(Margaret Daniel Primary School, Ashdown, AR)*

Filling the Shoes

Without being asked, staff members often fill in for someone who's late, absent, behind in work, or needs extra help. Give a special "Shoe Award" to those who "step up" to help others.

Hero Bulletin Board

Create a "Did You Ever Know You Were My Hero?" bulletin board. Staff members and students can write about the staff member(s) who inspired them and have become their hero. Read the entries each morning during the announcements while playing "The Wind Beneath My Wings."

 ## POSITIVE ATTITUDE

Attitude Certificates

Make *Good Attitude* certificates and give them to staff members or building coaches. When staff members see a colleague displaying a positive attitude, they can award the certificate to that person, who then puts his or her name on the back of the certificate and passes it along to another colleague when appropriate. *(Lima Senior High School, Lima, OH)*

You have been caught with a GOOD ATTITUDE.

TAG, YOU'RE IT!

Put your name on the back and pass this on to the next person caught with a good attitude.

Return to a building coach by _____.

MVP (Most Valuable Participant)

There are some people who are always there to help, calm the seas, contribute, offer suggestions, etc. Recognize them at the start of the school year when all staff members are present (or at another very public place) by dedicating the meeting or event to them. Write a proclamation that explains why they deserve the honor.

> Three billion people on the face of the earth go to bed hungry every night, but four billion people go to bed every night hungry for a simple word of encouragement and recognition.
>
> —*Cavett Robert, Founder of the National Speakers Association*

SCHOOL ACHIEVEMENT

Superior Staff

Some states rate schools each year; "superior" is the highest rating. If the school receives such a rating, be proud out loud. This gives the staff bragging rights, so provide them with achievement recognition items. Start by giving staff

members tote bags with the school mascot and "Superior School" printed on them. Later give matching T-shirts and lanyards. What's next? School spirit socks! *(Ross Elementary School, Milford, DE)*

BOB Award

Each marking period give a **BOB** pin to staff members who "**B**end **O**ver **B**ackwards" to achieve the goals set for the school and students. Anyone can recommend a staff member for the award. Take photos of the recipients and post them on the bulletin board.

Visible Difference Award

Give recognition to staff members who excel in their fields and make a visible difference in an area such as student achievement.

WILSON HALL

Halls of Fame

Name rooms and halls in honor of staff members whose students have the most improved test scores each year.

Chapter 2
Group Recognition

GENERAL RECOGNITION

The Brush Off

On snowy days, leave the building before other staff members and brush off the snow on their windshields.
(Gentiva Health Services, Kalamazoo, MI)

Seeing Clearly Now

During the day, wash the front windshield of staff member's cars and leave a note saying, "Our students' success is clearly in sight!"

Help Has Arrived

Give each staff member a **"One-Day Helper Pass"** in which student, parent, or community volunteers provide help with needed classroom activities.

"Supplies" Party

It's no secret that teachers spend a lot of their own money on classroom supplies. To help offset this expense, hold a surprise "Supplies Party." Ask parents, businesses, vendors, etc., to provide supply items from which staff members can choose for their classes.

Variation 1: Fill plastic storage boxes with stickers and other supplies and a give one box to each teacher.

Variation 2: Give each person a coupon for a $50 warehouse order to requisition classroom supplies. Attach a note to the order form that says **"The best resource in the school is YOU"** or **"We are fortunate to have a 'supply' of excellent staff members in our school."**

Switch Day

It's true that you really don't appreciate others until you walk in their shoes. Announce to the staff that on a designated day, they are to have lesson plans and all related materials on their desks as though they were going to be absent and a substitute teacher was to take over the class for a specific day.

List all the classrooms and write each teacher's name on a slip of paper. On the designated day, put all the teachers' names in a container for a drawing. Assemble the staff and draw one name at a time. Match each name to a classroom the person is to take for the day. The physical education teacher may now be teaching English or a third grade teacher may now be teaching kindergarten. Visit each of the classrooms and take pictures of the teachers in their new environment. At the end of the day, ask staff members to identify what they learned about teaching in a different department, subject area, grade level, etc. Share the results at the next staff meeting.

Variation: Have the staff members trade classrooms with teachers two levels above or below the grade level they teach. After the switch, have staff members form small groups and share their experiences. This helps dispel the "grass is always greener" image of other grade levels. You can also arrange to have staff members switch with teachers at other schools.

We Treasure Our Staff

Have the administrators dress up in pirate costumes—big, feathered hats, swords, and boots. Hold a surprise event to let the staff know they're "treasured." You can make this very elaborate with a treasure box full of donated items such as gift certificates, coupons, small gifts, etc., in which staff members individually select the "treasure" of their choice, or it could be filled with chocolate coins wrapped in gold foil.

We're "Jazzed Up" About Our Staff

Have the administrators dress up in Mardi Gras–themed clothing—lots of beads, masks, and costumes. Hold a surprise celebration to show staff members how "jazzed" you are about their work: have Dixieland music playing and serve a New Orleans–style meal or a snack of pralines, gumbo, crawfish, red beans and rice, or jambalaya.

Multimedia Presentation

Prepare multimedia presentations featuring a particular staff member. Examples include:

Version 1: Baby pictures through current photos with the honoree's favorite music in the background.

Version 2: Compare the staff member to a cartoon character (e.g., if someone loves to hunt, compare that person to Elmer Fudd. Use the staff member's name as a caption below a photo of the cartoon character.)
(Alonsa School, Alonsa, Manitoba, Canada)

Announce the Appreciation

Periodically put educational quotes in the morning PA announcements and in memos; this reminds people of the impact educators have on children and society. Examples of appropriate quotes include:

I think that the greatest success of any life is that moment when a teacher touches a child's heart and it is never again the same . . . Everything America is or ever hopes to be depends upon what happens in our school's classrooms.
—FROSTY TROY, EDITOR, Oklahoma Observer

There is a place in America to take a stand: it is public education. It is the underpinning of our cultural and political system. It is the great common ground. Public education after all is the engine that moves us as a society toward a common destiny . . . It is in public education that the American dream begins to take shape.
—TOM BROKAW, NEWS ANCHOR

There's no word in the language I revere more than 'teacher.' My heart sings when a kid refers to me as his teacher, and it always has. I've honored myself and the entire family of man by becoming a teacher.
—PAT CONROY, AUTHOR, Prince of Tides

Teachers teach because they care. Teaching young people is what they do best. It requires long hours, patience, and care.
—HORACE MANN, EDUCATOR

Spread the Guests

When you have a large meeting, avoid having a VIP or head table. Rather, seat the administrators, board members, and guests among staff members so they can interact with each other. Everyone in the room is a VIP!

Building Makeover

Honor the staff by providing them with a nice lounge. Organize volunteers to give the room a new look with fresh paint, decorations, curtains, framed artwork, and lots of creativity. Celebrate the completion of the revamped lounge by holding an Open House.

Principal's Sign

Hang a sign in the school office that has this message from the principal *(San Lorenzo Unified School District, San Lorenzo, CA).*

> # Please be kind to the people who work here. I love every one of them. — *The Principal*

"Note"worthy Recognition

At the start of the year, ask staff members to tell you the name of their favorite song. Download these songs and make a staff CD.

Variation: Have members of the choir or band serenade each staff member periodically throughout the year and perform the "favorites" on the list.

FOOD REWARDS

Appreciative Sayings

Looking Forward to Monday Morning included many
ideas for expressing appreciation, including attaching fun
phrases to food items to be given to staff members at meetings, placed on their desks or in their mailboxes, etc. Since
that book was published, I've asked numerous U.S. and
Canadian educators to share some of the phrases they've
created when giving various food items. Below are some
of the responses:

Tabasco Red Hot Candy

Our staff is "red hot"!
You really know how to "fire up" your students!
Our school is on top because your teaching is so "hot"!
When you're hot, you're hot! Thanks for _____

M&M's

Marvelous & Motivated
Marvelous & Magnificent—that's what you are!
Monday Morning Motivators
Marvelous Monday—Have a great week!

M&M's Peanut Candy

We're nuts about our staff!

Doublemint Gum

We "chews" you!
Our staff "sticks" together.
Teaching with you is double the fun.
Stick to it!

Treasures Candy

You're one of our "treasures."
You're truly a "treasure" on our campus.
We "treasure" the work you do.
We discovered a "treasure" when we hired YOU!

Nestlé Crunch Candy Bar

Thank you for your help at "crunch" time.

Tootsie Roll Candy

You play a huge "role" in the success of our school!

100 Grand Candy Bar

You're worth 100 Grand, but this is all I can afford.
100 Grand does not suffice for the 100 Grand things you do.
For all you do—here's 100 Grand for you!
Life is Grand—so are You!

Gummy Bear Candy

Thanks for being so "bearie" special.
You make bad days "bearable."
Thanks for "bearing" the extra load.
Big bear hugs for all you do.

Hugs Candy

*Thanks for **H**elping **U**s **G**ive to **S**tudents.*
***H**uge **U**ndertaking. **G**reat **S**uccess!*
For all you do . . . This Hug's for you!
A handful of Hugs for a Great day!

5th Avenue Candy Bar

Our staff is first class!

Promise Candy

We "promise" to stand by you.

Thanks for fulfilling the "promise" of helping students learn.

This "promises" to be a good day/week.

Thanks for trying "promising" ideas in your classroom.

Mint Candy

Thanks for the commit"mint" you make to our school.

Nutter Butter Cookies

There's "nutter butter" than our staff!

Heathbar Bites Candy

You take the "bite" out of _____ (e.g., state tests).

Being Involved Together, Everyone Succeeds!

"Bites" of appreciation!

Cup of Pudding

Thanks for "pudding" up with _____.

Starburst

*We are "bursting" with excitement over
    your success (or talent).*

You are a "star" with us!

*Thanks for being a "star" with
    your "burst" of enthusiasm.*

Our faculty is "bursting" with "stars."

Our staff reaches for the stars!

Room Service

Decorate a cart and stock it with treats—lemonade and cookies or hot chocolate, coffee and donuts, soft drinks, etc. Dress up as a chef or formal waiter and deliver the treats to each classroom in recognition of the teachers' hard work. Using nonplastic utensils, china plates, glassware, and cloth napkins are appreciated special touches. *(Breeze Hill Elementary School, Vista, CA, Parker School, Galveston, TX, Miller Grove School, Cumby, TX, and Carroll Independent School District, Southlake, TX)*

Cooking Up Appreciation

If you love to cook, share your talent at a hectic time such as Parent-Teacher Conference week. Create your own special day such as "_____ (Your School's Name) Meatball Day." Let staff members know you're going to prepare and serve them meatballs along with rolls, salad, and dessert for lunch. Wear a chef's hat and serve the gourmet delights. Other special days could be Salad Bar or Pasta Bar Day. Saving staff members from the extra work of preparing their own lunch is a way of showing your appreciation. *(Moreau Hall Elementary School, Easton, MA)*

The Day After

Night events are common at schools (e.g., parent-teacher conferences, Open Houses, etc.). Preparing for the following day often is difficult. Provide lunch for staff members the day after the night event, so they don't have to worry about packing a lunch. *(Samuel Smith School, Burlington, NJ)*

Dessert Day

Ask each staff member to tell you what his or her favorite dessert is. Then, have parent or community volunteers prepare those delicacies and present them to the individual staff members to take home.

Candy Store

Decorate the staff lounge like an old fashioned candy store and have lots of candy in jars for staff members to enjoy. Put up a sign that says, "For Our Sweet Staff."

Apple Mania

Have an apple event in which you serve treats such as home-made applesauce, apple pie, fritters, caramel apples, apple suckers, etc. Provide fresh apples as well, and hot apple cider if the weather's right. Decorate the area with apple pictures.

"Appeeling" Teachers

Give each teacher an apple with the following note attached to it. *(Villa Rica Middle School, Temple, GA)*

You plant the seeds of wisdom with patience and concern.
And your efforts all bear fruit as your students grow and learn.
You offer them good food for thought and you care right to the core.
And there's just no better teacher than the one this apple is for!

You are My Gyro!

To recognize the achievement of a special project, have a surprise gyro or hero sandwich lunch. Display a banner with "You are My Gyro/Hero" on it. *(Gentiva Health Services, Kalamazoo, MI)*

Coffee Day

Arrange to have a coffee van in the staff parking lot before school and during lunch. Give staff members coupons they can use to purchase beverages.

Faux Fire Drill

On a non-student day when the weather's nice, have a fire drill. When staff members assemble in the parking lot, have coffee and donuts waiting for them as a fun surprise. *(Glenway School, Dominion City, Manitoba, Canada)*

SYMBOLS OF RECOGNITION

The Medium is the Message

Find small items at the Dollar Store or in novelty catalogs such as Oriental Trading Company. Think up creative ways of expressing appreciation using the item you've selected. As is mentioned under Appreciative Sayings in the Food Rewards section, U.S. and Canadian educators came up with many phrases to accompany items for staff members. Their suggestions included:

Notepad

We are taking "note" of the great job you are doing!

You are a helpful reminder of why I love my job.

You did a "noteworthy" job.

You "pad" the success of our school.

Packet of Aspirin

You take out the pain of _____

You are "aspiring."

You've done my heart good!

You're the remedy for all aches!

You're better for my heart than aspirin.

Battery

Your energy keeps on going and going.

Thanks for your enthusiasm. You energize the whole staff.

Your classroom was really charged today.

You are an "ever ready" teacher!

Pen

In my o"pen"ion, this staff is the best!

Thanks for helping write the futures of our students.

Pushpins or Tacks

Thanks for the extra push.

Thanks for being so "tackful."

Thanks for sticking together on this project.

Stick with your ideas!

Small Mirror

This person is a very special teacher.

Plastic Sunglasses

Attach a note: "Our students' futures are so bright, we have to wear shades" and play "The Future's So Bright, I Gotta Wear Shades" by Timbuk3 throughout the day.

Lightbulb-Shaped Eraser

Thanks for "turning on the light" of student achievement.

Candle

You light up the lives of our students.

Flower Candle

You light up the lives of the kids and help them blossom and grow.

Snail Soap or Candle

Unlike the snail, you are quick in the race toward student achievement.

Measuring Tape

By every measure, you're GREAT!

You more than measure up.

Few measure up to you!

Band-Aid

Together we can heal any boo-boos.
I'm sorry if I hurt your feelings.
You are the best teacher's aid!
Here's to you for coming through that "scrape" on top.

Snow Globe

S'now secret—you're Great!
There's "snowbody" like you.
You really shake things up!

GIFTS OF TIME

There just doesn't seem to be enough hours in the day! Staff members often lament about not being able to get everything done they want to do—or not even having time to catch their breath.

During my presentations I conduct an informal survey of rewards the audience would like to receive for good attendance. "Gifts of time" is the top-ranked reward— in every state and in every type of audience. Staff members value time with their families and flexibility in schedules. Discretionary time at work is also valued; student-free and rest/ relaxation times are so necessary.

An educator in London shared that during recess, the headmaster supervises the students so the teachers can have tea. How lovely!

Tea Time

On a given day(s), have recess times covered and have *Tea Time* in which beverages and pastries are served.

Read Aloud

Have the principal, itinerant staff, or counselor read
to the students for 30 minutes; this provides a short
break for teachers, and gives the students
a different presence in the classroom.

Out to Lunch

Once a month, select staff members to go out for a 90-minute
lunch. A different group is selected each week; the groups
change every month. The remaining educators cover the
classrooms for those who are "out to lunch." This is an
excellent way for staff members to get to know each other
and relax. *(Tenderfoot Primary School, Sanger, TX)*

Lunch and Shop

Arrange for businesses and vendors to display their products during the lunch times so that staff members can shop
without leaving school. This is especially helpful prior to
holiday periods.

Photocopying Help

Provide volunteers to do provide photocopying assistance
on given days.

Chapter 3
Individual Recognition

SPECIAL RECOGNITION

Golden Glow Award

Contact local television stations and ask them to feature staff members in their programming. Reporters can interview the staff members in their school setting. Give certificates to the featured staff members; the names for these awards could be the *Golden Glow Award, Class Act Award, Excellence in Teaching Award,* or *Show and Tell.*

> Everybody likes a compliment.
>
> – *Abraham Lincoln*

Educator of the Week

Version 1: Recognize a teacher in a morning assembly each week, and encourage students to cheer loudly for that person. The teacher receives a Teacher of the Week "parking cone" and is able to park in a parking place of his or her choice for the week. *(Tenderfoot Primary School, Sanger, TX)*

Version 2: Recognize the Educator of the Week each Monday morning. Include the person's name during the morning announcements and display his or her name on the school's marquee. Ask gifted and talented students to interview the educator and share this information during the morning announcements later that week. Ask the honoree to give some words of wisdom during announcements as well. Hang a huge star outside of the person's classroom or office for the week. Create a small bulletin board display

about the honoree to help others learn more about this person. On the last day of the month, the PTO could provide lunch for the staff members recognized that month. *(Meyer Elementary School, Richmond, TX)*

Headline News

At the end of the year, hold a drawing for a large prize, such as a trip to a fun locale. Staff members get a chance to win each time their name is mentioned in the district's newsletter during the year.

GENERAL RECOGNITION

"Whale" Done

Purchase a stuffed whale and make a sign for it that says "Whale Done." Then make a bulletin board with the same title and cut out miniature pictures of whales, leaving room on the paper for written comments. When a staff member does something worthy of recognition, publicly acknowledge the action by announcing it over the P.A. system or sharing the information at a staff meeting. Give the recipient the whale to keep until someone else earns it. Anyone (colleague, student, administrator, etc.) can give this award.

Write the award winner's name and action on the paper whale and post on the "Whale Done" bulletin board. Keep the names posted all year; start the program over when school begins again in the fall. A person can receive this award numerous times throughout the year.

> Individual commitment to a group effort—that is what makes a team work, a company work, a society work, a civilization work.
>
> —*Vince Lombardi*

Teacher Feature

Create a bulletin board in a conspicuous location, and periodically feature information about staff members on the board, including pictures and a profile listing favorite quotes, background, family, hobbies, etc.

Culinary Delights

Name sandwiches or entrees served in the cafeteria after staff members, (e.g., "Mrs. Hodges' Hearty Hoagies," "Mr. Martin's Marvelous Macaroni," etc.)

"Egg"cellent Staff Members

Fill plastic eggs with candy and treats. When great things happen, attach special messages to the eggs and put them in staff members' mailboxes. Examples are "You are an Egg-cellent teacher" or "You are Egg-citing to work with." Most words starting with "ex" will work—exceptional, extra special, experienced, exuberant, etc.

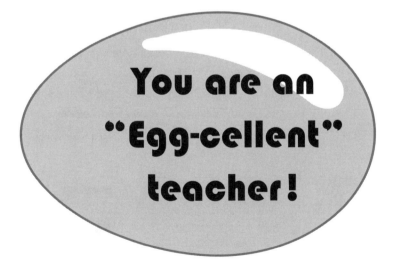

Pat on the Back

Trace a shirt on a piece of construction paper—one for each staff person. Write a staff member's name on each of the shirts. Make hand patterns and give everyone a supply equal to the number of staff members. Have each staff member write something positive about each of his or her colleagues on the paper hands, and then return them.

A Pat on the Back for . . .

Voice Mail Appreciation

Call staff members' home phone numbers and leave positive voice messages on their answering machines. The messages can be words of thanks, recognition, etc.

Honor Walls

Make a display outside each staff member's work area that gives information about them, including their picture, diplomas, credentials, awards, etc. *(State of Alabama Department of Education, Montgomery, AL)*

Summer Messages

Keep in touch over the summer. Send out group e-mails when there's news in the district or school. Send individual, personalized e-mails, too, to let staff members know you're thinking about them and are looking forward to seeing them again in the fall.

Special Box

Sometimes people just need a reminder that another person cares. Cut out a small block of wood and wrap it with paper and ribbon. Attach the following poem to the package and give one to colleagues who need it throughout the year. (*Author comment:* I made one of these boxes for my mother and when she died, she had it with her. That made me feel really good!)
(*Debra Macklin, Quincy, MI*)

Whenever you feel lonely
Whenever you feel bad
Whenever you are anxious
Or just a little sad

Hold this gift I give you
It's filled with love and hope
It's everything you'll ever need
To endure hard times and cope

Please leave the wrapping on it
Don't remove the bow
It must remain undisturbed
For when you're feeling low

The contents aren't solid
They don't weigh very much
But all it takes to make it work
Is a little faith and your gentle touch

This box is very special
I share it now with you
May everything that's wonderful
Touch everything you do.

One of a Kind

Purchase a jigsaw puzzle with enough pieces so that each staff person gets one. Put a motivational message such as the one shown on a sheet of paper and glue one puzzle piece to each sheet. Give it to staff members at times appropriate to the message.

Each of us is a piece of this great puzzle, interlocking with one another to make one complete picture. Even though each is different, without our piece of the puzzle, our school would not be complete.

Remember, it is through our relationships and connectedness with one another that we will make a force so strong that each of us will positively change the lives of children and one another forever.

WRITTEN APPRECIATION

Journal It

Place a journal in the staff lounge or other location where staff members congregate. Encourage them to write an entry in the journal whenever they see something that makes them smile, warms their hearts, or makes them proud to be in education. This can be done for a designated week and the results read at a staff meeting, or it can be ongoing. At the end of the year, compile the entries and give a copy to each staff member.

After-Hours Praise

After staff members have left for the day, visit various classrooms. On the white board, write notes to the teachers complimenting them, the students' work, etc. This is a nice way for them to start the next day.

Post-it Note Praise

Surprise a staff member with a display of Post-it notes with words of recognition or praise on them.

Thank-U-Grams

Have envelopes and stationery printed so that you can send "Thank-U-Grams" in recognition of the good work that staff members have done. *(Nixa R-II School District, Nixa, MO)*

Web Appreciation

Encourage parents, students, graduates, and community members to post appreciative messages and pictures on the district's Web site. For example:

Staff Member Appreciation

Name of Staff Member _____

School Location _____

Year You Graduated or Current Grade Level _____

You can reach me at _____

Message:

Section II

Fun Ways to Spend Work Days

We do not laugh because we are happy.
Rather, we are happy because we laugh.
—William James

Chapter 4
From the Beginning

NEW YEAR STARTERS

Summer Highs and Lows

At the beginning of the school year, ask staff members to stand and join hands. Each person shares a "high" and "low" event of the summer. Everyone quickly catches up on their colleagues' lives; people can find out more details as desired. *(Park Elementary School, Corning, AR)*

Summer "Whines"

Have staff members share the whining they heard from their children over the summer. Examples include, *There's nothing to do, I'm bored, We're hot, We don't have to go to bed early in the summer,* etc.

> May all your troubles last as long as your New Year's resolutions.

Back to the Grind

Many staff members return to school before their contracted start day. Let them know that food and drinks will be available for them throughout the day. Arrange to have some student helpers available as well (if possible).

You might also give each person a coupon for a "Welcome Back Bag." Staff members in attendance before the school year begins can then bring the coupon to the office, catch up on the summer's activities, and receive a bag of goodies.

Lend a Hand

Set a date and e-mail staff members to participate in a voluntary Lend a Hand Day. Staff members come in before school starts to help new teachers set up their rooms and get acclimated to the new school.

Road Rally

Divide the staff members into groups of four or five members so they can ride together in a car. Make a list of people they need to find and have their picture taken with. Set a limit of a certain amount of time. Each picture is assigned points, for example:

- Picture with the mayor = 25 points
- Picture with a former principal = 30 points
- Picture with a security guard at the university = 20 points

Each team makes a video of their meetings and brings it back to the school. The videos are judged but not shown until the last teacher day of the year. Prizes are given for the most points, the most creative, etc.

Mystery Trips

Plan a staff mystery trip before students return from summer break. Some districts have this trip on a regular contracted day, but many have it before the staff's contractual period. Everyone is welcome; participation is voluntary. Let staff members know where to meet, the start time, and approximate ending time. Provide suggestions for what to wear. Examples of trips include taking the staff to a movie, historical tour, blueberry picking, or a shell hunt (followed by a seafood meal).

One district made arrangements with a mom and pop restaurant to have the staff work in the restaurant for the day. Some cooked while others waited and bused tables. They even dined on their culinary creations. Participants had fun and learned new skills.

Another district planned an overnight camping trip. The staff members were told what to wear and bring, and that the activity would involve an overnight. The group cooked on a campfire, sang, and toasted marshmallows. (However, two members were unhappy with the camping arrangements, and were taken to a nearby hotel. Keep in mind that this type of event may not be a big hit with everyone.)

Start of the Year Relays

Divide the staff members into teams of 5-6 people. Hold relays representing start of the school year activities such as:

Game 1   Get Ready for School – dress for school relay

Game 2   Breakfast Relay – blindfolded feeding relay

Game 3   Washing Up – shaving a balloon relay

Game 4   Get to School – tricycle riding relay

Game 5   Don't Forget Your Backpack – stuffing school supplies into a backpack relay

Award ribbons and prizes such as classroom supplies to the winners.

New Staff Member Shower

Hold a shower for new staff members. The gifts that are given are items that can be used in their classrooms such as bulletin board displays, card file of ideas, etc.

Coupon Books

At the start of the school year, give each staff member a coupon book with coupons that can be used throughout the year. For example:

- Wear Jeans for the Day Coupon
- Leave Early Coupon
- Arrive at 8:00 A.M. Coupon
- Redeem for a dozen cookies from the cafeteria Coupon
- Free Cafeteria Lunch Coupon
- Free Car Wash Coupon

Bunco Party

Before getting down to the mundane start of the school year activities, allow the staff to spend a little time together after the summer break. For an hour, host a bunco party and award prizes to the winners.

Letter to Yourself

Have staff members write goals for themselves in areas such as curriculum, classroom management, parent communications, etc. Have them also set a goal for colleague relationships and support.

Put the goals into envelopes with the staff member's name on the front, seal the envelopes, and then store them until the second semester. The person who wrote the goals is the only one who'll read them.

At mid-year, distribute the envelopes to the staff members to review and reflect on what they have done toward achieving their goals.

The envelopes are resealed and stored away by the principal. At the end of the year, give the staff members their respective envelopes containing the goals, and ask them to review for reflection and goal setting for the following school year.

> A commitment is a heartfelt promise to yourself from which you will not back down.

Survival Kit

Make a Survival Kit for each staff member by placing the following instructions in a bag, along with the items mentioned.

Survival Kit for Educators

TOOTHPICK   To remind you **to pick out the good qualities** in your students.

RUBBER BAND   To remind you to **be flexible** throughout the day.

PAPER CLIP   To remind you to **hold it** all together.

ERASER   To remind you to start each day with **a clean slate**.

BAND AID   To remind you to **heal hurt feelings**—yours or a student's.

CLAY   To remind you that you are **molding futures**.

LIFESAVER   For always **being there** when your students need you.

MARBLE   To **replace those we lose** from time to time.

MINT   To remind you that you are **worth a mint**.

TEA BAG   To remind you to **relax and take time for yourself**.

PIPE CLEANER	**Flexibility** is important for a successful year.
RICK RACK	This year will be full of **ups and downs**, but it will all smooth out.
MATCHES	For those days when you feel you need to **light a fire** under the students.
WIGGLY EYE	**Keep an eye on the students** to determine how to best help them.
BATTERY	Like the Energizer Bunny, this will keep you **going, and going, and going**.
ANIMAL CRACKER	For when you think your **job is a zoo**.
JINGLE BELL	**Ring** for help when you need it.
PRESENT	Remember, our students are a **gift** to us.
CANDY BAR	Use when you need a **"sweet escape."**
SMILEY STICKER	Wear a **happy face**.
SNOWFLAKE	When all else fails, pray for a **Snow Day!**
FLOWER POT	We are here to **plant the seeds** of knowledge.
CLOTHESPIN	**Hang** in there!
HOLE REINFORCERS	Don't forget to **reinforce each other's efforts**.

School Lanyards

Purchase commercially made school lanyards for each staff member. Make them in your school's colors and embroider the school's name on it. Personalize each one by embroidering on the first and last name of each staff member. Staff members can attach their school identification badges, keys, whistle, etc. on them. *(Breeze Hill Elementary School, Vista, CA)*

Welcome Back Notes

Leave a personal note on all staff members' workstations welcoming them back and wishing them the best of school years.

CHOOSE A THEME

At the start of the year, staff members select a theme for the year. Activities, meetings, celebrations, etc., center on this theme. Examples that have been selected by schools include:

Make it Happen!

Work as a TEAM!

Put on your big girl panties and deal with it!

We don't care how _____ (state capital) does it; we have success this way!

The Journey Begins With Us

One school selected the theme, **The Journey Begins With Us**. To create a visual to go along with the theme, each staff member decorated a star to symbolize that the staff members were all-stars. The stars were used to create a paper quilt and displayed at the district office. *(Pasadena Unified School District, Pasadena, CA)*

Ronald is an All-Star!

Knock Your Socks Off This Year!

Another district selected the theme, *Knock Your Socks Off This Year!* The principal made a banner incorporating the theme. The staff members had to run through it and break it to enter the staff meeting room. When inside, a pair of socks was on each chair with their school logo on it.

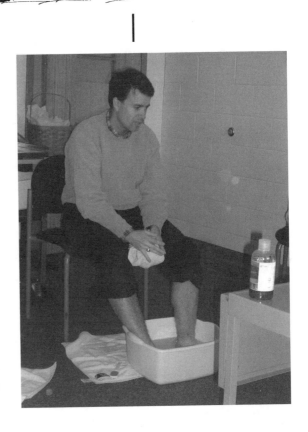

Later in the year another activity was held that was consistent with the theme, **Knock Your Socks Off**. As they approached the time for testing, the principal planned a *Peppermint Soak*. Based on the premise that the aroma of peppermint may help release tension and dissipate fatigue, arrangements were made with a Body Shop consultant to do peppermint foot soaks for the entire staff. Staff members soaked and scrubbed their feet, applied foot gel and lotion, and enjoyed a peppermint mask. It was an awesome event and a great destresser prior to the tests.

The plans for the following year is the theme, **Let's Roll With It!** The school has many football fans, so footballs will be incorporated into the activities. (*Ross Elementary School, Milford, DE*)

Joe Lingo of Ross Elementary in Milford, DE, enjoys a peppermint soak at the end of the day.

Take the Dare

Take the Dare is another theme. It's easier and more comfortable to be stable and stagnate than it is to move out of your comfort zone and try something new. Rearview thinking (looking in the rearview mirror and doing things the way they were done in the past) has not served education well. Educators have to dare to be different—to try new things. Encourage the staff to really live this theme throughout the year.

Choose to Fly

Choose to Fly is a theme based on the book, Dumbo. Summarize the story of *Dumbo* for staff members: a baby elephant is born to Mrs. Jumbo, a circus elephant. The baby has enormous ears and is teased and called "Dumbo." His mother goes on a rampage trying to defend her baby and is locked away. Dumbo is left with only his friend, a mouse who uses a "magic feather" to convince the baby elephant to reach his full potential—to use his big ears so that he can fly.

Give each staff member a feather and remind them they, too, can fly this year. Incorporate the feather theme into awards and accomplishments throughout the year.

> Form the habit of saying 'yes' to a good idea. Then write down the reasons why it will work. There will always be plenty of people around you to tell you it won't work.
> —Gil Atkinson

Golden Staff Award

Go for the Gold

Use the Olympic theme for the year—*Go for the Gold*. Have awards such as Golden Staff Award and Funny/Fun Olympics.

Organize several fun events in which staff members compete. The "Olympics" can be an ongoing event or just a day of fun. Some events might include:

- **Broom baseball** — Bat with a broom rather than a bat and run the bases backwards.
- **Lay an egg** — Divide staff members into pairs and have them stand with their backs to each other. Place a raw egg between their backs and see if they can lay the egg on the ground without breaking it.
- **Dress-up relay** — Make two piles of the same type of clothing. Divide the staff into teams. Have the first person on each team race to put on all of the clothes in the pile —and then take them off. The next player then does the same. The team that dresses and undresses the fastest wins.

- **Find the rainbow** — Divide the staff into teams. Give each team a bag with a piece of paper with the colors of the rainbow (red, orange, yellow, green, blue, indigo, and violet) written on it. Each team is to find and put in the bag an object outside that matches each color. The winner is the first team to find objects that match all of the colors.
- **Foot golf** — Hit the ball with your foot rather than a golf club.
- **Hula-hoop relay** — Divide the staff into an even number of teams and provide a hula-hoop and a stick for each team. Devise a course for each team to follow. Start the relay by blowing a whistle; then each competitor rolls the hoop through the course and back by using either a hand or the stick. The hula-hoop is handed off to the next player. The relay continues until all of the players of one team complete the course.

GET ACQUAINTED ACTIVITIES

About Me

Divide the staff into groups. Give them a list of questions and have them share their answers with each other. Question could be as follows:

- What are your favorite pizza toppings?
- What is your pet peeve?
- If you could go anywhere for vacation, where would you go?
- How do you like to relax?
- What do you daydream about?
- What's your favorite summer activity?
- Where did you go to college?
- What makes you smile?

Creative Name Tags

Have an assortment of art materials available for staff members to use. Instruct them to create name tags that describe them without actually using their names. Divide the staff into groups and allow time for each person to explain his or her tag to the group. The tags should be worn throughout the day and serve as a conversation starter.

This Song's About ME!

Ask each staff member to submit their favorite song and a description of their interests, hobbies, number of children, college they attended, animals they own, etc. Each day one song and description are included as part of the announcements. Each class tries to guess which staff member is being described. The winners get a small prize (such as candy).

Get to Know Each Other Better via E-mail

Send this e-mail to a designated staff member to complete. That person then sends it on to another person to complete, until it has reached everyone on staff. It helps colleagues learn more about each other.

E-Mail Questionnaire

Name as it appears on your birth certificate:

Nicknames:

What was the last movie you saw in a theater?

Place of birth:

Favorite foods:

Have you ever loved someone so much
  it made you cry?

Have you been in a car accident?

Do you prefer croutons or bacon bits?

Favorite day of the week:

Favorite restaurant:

Favorite flower:

Favorite spectator sport:

Favorite drink:

Favorite ice cream:

Favorite fast food restaurant:

Before this one, from whom did you get your last e-mail?

In which store would you choose to max out your credit card?

What do you do most often when you are bored?

What is your normal bedtime?

What are your favorite TV shows?

Do you prefer Ford or Chevy?

What is your favorite color?

Do you prefer a lake, ocean, or river?

RETURN DIRECTIONS: Copy this entire e-mail and paste it onto a new e-mail that you will send. Change all of the answers so they apply to you. Then send it to a staff member who has not received the e-mail. In this way, you'll learn many little-known facts about your colleagues. Enjoy the discoveries!

Chapter 5

Staff Meetings

FUN-FILLED STAFF MEETINGS

Fun-Filled Staff Meetings

OK, answer honestly. Whether you are conducting or attending them, do you look forward to staff meetings? Or, to avoid them, do you try to schedule doctor or dentist appointments on those days? Have you ever thought of why you might be resisting staff meetings?

It could be that they just aren't *fun*—there isn't any motivation to look forward to them. One Fortune 500 company held weekly Monday morning meetings that the participants began to refer to as "Monday morning beatings." It was a time to ridicule and tear into the staff. It was very hard for that team to look forward to Monday mornings.

5 Minutes of FUN

Make a calendar of the dates of upcoming staff meetings. Ask each staff person to sign up to lead a fun activity at the start of the meeting. It should be brief and should bring

"I need the formula for better attendance at staff meetings."

the staff together through laughter, entertainment, mental stimulation, etc. When "playtime" is over and people are feeling happy, energized, and enthusiastic, the business part of the meeting can begin.

Some people will immediately know what type of activity they want to lead; others may struggle with this "assignment." Those people may want to use some of the activities suggested here.

Note: It may take several staff meetings to complete some activities, while others will just take the first few minutes of the meeting.

A-Z Recognition

The leader starts the activity by calling out the letter "A." A volunteer staff member stands up and says a complimentary statement about a colleague that starts with the letter "A." Example: "A is for Jane because she always has a great **A**ttitude." Then proceed to "B," and someone gives another compliment, such as "B is for Cindi because she **B**usts her **B**uns to help others."

Show and Tell

Each staff member signs up to share a "show and tell" activity with the rest of the staff. Such activities might be the introduction of a new pet, hobbies, recognitions, story, project, etc. *(Gentiva Health Services, Kalamazoo, MI)*

Joke of the Day

Staff members sign up to tell a joke at the start of the meeting. *Laugh Lines for Educators* is the perfect resource for this activity. Make sure the jokes are in good taste. *(Gentiva Health Services, Kalamazoo, MI)*

Spoons

Give a metal spoon to each person, and have them try to balance it on their nose and chin. Be sure to have a camera handy!

Decades of Fun

Remember the "good old days"? The days we can't fully remember—or totally forget. The ones we often relive and laugh about. Have the staff divide into groups by decades, either the decade in which they were in their mid- to late-teens, or in their 20's. Assign a staff meeting for each group to plan using the events and fads of their particular decade. The event could focus on the music (sing-along, name that tune, dance contest), food, dress, movies, trivia, etc., of the period.

1950s

Music
"Rock Around the Clock"
"Blue Suede Shoes"
"Mack the Knife"

TV Shows
I Love Lucy
The Honeymooners
American Bandstand

Fads
Hoola Hoops

1960s

Music

"Loco-motion"

"The Twist"

"Surfin' USA"

"I Want to Hold Your Hand"

"Mrs. Robinson"

"Blowin' in the Wind"

The British Invasion

The Motown Sound

Woodstock Music Festival

TV Shows

Candid Camera

Beverly Hillbillies

Bonanza

The Man From U.N.C.L.E.

Gilligan's Island

Jeopardy

Star Trek

Laugh-in

The Dating Game

Bewitched

The Mod Squad

Hootenanny

Movies/Theater

Hair

007 – James Bond movies

Pink Panther

Mary Poppins

Funny Girl

1970s

Music

"Bridge Over Troubled Water"
"American Pie"
"Tie a Yellow Ribbon"
"Stayin' Alive"

TV Shows

All in the Family
The Waltons
The Partridge Family
Saturday Night Live
Charlie's Angels
Three's Company
Roots
Mork and Mindy
Dallas
Taxi
Fantasy Island

Movies

Young Frankenstein
Close Encounters
Grease
Star Wars
Saturday Night Fever
Rocky
Alien

Other

First VCR introduced by Sony
First home video game: Pong from Atari

1980s

Music

"Let's Get Physical"
"Billie Jean"
Theme from *Flash Dance*
"Born in the USA"
"Don't Worry, Be Happy"

TV Shows

Diff'rent Strokes
The Love Boat
Dynasty
Cheers
Murphy Brown
Roseanne
The Wonder Years
Dallas

Movies

Caddyshack
Airplane!
Raiders of the Lost Ark
E.T.
Tootsie
Ghostbusters
Back to the Future
Dirty Dancing

Fads

Pac-Man
Cabbage Patch Dolls
Trivial Pursuit
Nintendo

1990s

Music

"I Will Always Love You"
"Macarena"
"Candle in the Wind"
"Livin' La Vida Loca"
"All I Wanna Do"

TV Shows

The Simpsons
Full House
Spin City
Frasier
Melrose Place
Friends
Mad About You
Ally McBeal
Everybody Loves Raymond
Who Wants to be a Millionaire?

Movies

Home Alone
Pretty Woman
Beauty and the Beast
Sleepless in Seattle
Forrest Gump
The Lion King
Toy Story
There's Something About Mary
Austin Powers

Line Dancing

There's a little cowboy/cowgirl in all of us just waiting to get out. Select a simple line dance such as the electric slide. Give the staff members dance lessons and let them practice the steps. Then let the dancing begin!

I Never . . .

Start by giving each person several "markers" such as popcorn, beans, pennies, or toothpicks. Form a circle, or multiple circles if the group is large. Someone starts the game by telling the group one thing he or she has never done (e.g., flown on an airplane, broken a bone, eaten snails, had a shoeshine, etc.). Anyone who has done this activity must give the person a marker. After going around the circle several times, the person with the most markers wins and gets a prize.

5 Minutes of Song

If you have ever attended a Kiwanis or other service organization meeting, you will have noticed that they start their meetings with songs. Start your staff meeting with high-energy, fun songs that people can sing along to. Pick songs that are about holidays or seasons.

A "GASP" Aspect

Select a panel of judges. Ask staff members to share experiences from their own lives that would make the judges "gasp." These can be gruesome, suspenseful, amazing, etc. Each week, select three volunteers to share their stories at the staff meeting. The judges determine if one, two, or all three are worthy of a "GASP." Small prizes or gift certificates can be awarded to the winners.

5 Minutes of Movement

Lead the staff in a few minutes of stretching, relaxation, or other stress-reducing movement before the staff meeting begins.

Left Brain! Right Brain!

After staff members are seated, tell them to lift their right foot off the floor and make clockwise circles. Now, while doing this, tell them to draw the number 6 in the air with their right hand once. Their foot will change direction, and there's nothing they can do about it.

Sing—or Butcher— Your Favorite Song

Have a staff karaoke session (this could take several meetings). You could also incorporate a sing-along activity in which all staff members participate.

Dream Careers

Ask each person to write down his or her dream career, by answering this question: "If you weren't in education, what would you do?" Collect the answers and put them on a summary sheet. Give each staff member a copy of the compiled list and a list of the staff members. Have them try to match up the answers with the people. Reveal the answers at the meeting and give a prize to the person who has the most correct answers. Give a boobie prize, too. *(Rebecca Steele, Kalamazoo, MI)*

Balloons

Put a balloon on each chair. When staff members sit down, they have to pop the balloons. Watch them wiggle, squirm, and laugh.

Educational Trivia

Make trivia game questions about teachers from popular movies such as *Dead Poet's Society; Stand and Deliver; To Sir, With Love; Goodbye Mr. Chips; Dangerous Minds; Pay it Forward; October Sky; High School High; Summer School.*

What's in Your Bag?

In advance of the meeting tell the staff to put up to 20 items found in their desks, wallets, brief cases, and purses into a bag and bring them to the meeting. Using the items brought, have a contest to see who . . .

- Has the largest number of people in a picture
- Has the oldest coin
- Has the smallest pencil
- Has the highest number of calories in a single item (candy bar, chips, etc.)

Give prizes to the winners of each category.

Manly Chick Flick Movie Reviews

When a "chick flick" movie is released, ask for a male staff member to volunteer to see it. Give him two tickets to attend the movie, and then report back at the staff meeting with a review of the movie.

College Fight Songs

Survey the staff to determine where they went to college. Make a CD of snippets of the fight songs from each school. Play the music and when the staff members recognize their college fight song, they stand up and clap and/or sing the words.

Interesting Facts

Cut out the following facts. Give each one to a different person. Go around the room and have each person read his or her fact. (Because there are so many, it would be best to do this activity over the course of several staff meetings; otherwise people could lose interest due to information overload.)

A dime has 118 ridges around the edge.

A cat has 32 muscles in each ear.

A crocodile cannot stick out its tongue.

A dragonfly has a life span of 24 hours.

A goldfish has a memory span of three seconds.

A "jiffy" is an actual unit of time for 1/100th of a second.

A shark is the only fish that can blink with both eyes.

A snail can sleep for three years.

Al Capone's business card said he was a used furniture dealer.

All 50 states are listed across the top of the Lincoln Memorial on the back of the $5 bill.

Almonds are a member of the peach family.

An ostrich's eye is bigger than its brain.

Butterflies taste with their feet.

> If you don't learn to laugh at trouble, you won't have anything to laugh at when you grow old.
> —Edward W. Howe

Cats have over 100 vocal sounds. Dogs only have about 10.

"Dreamt" is the only English word that ends in the letters "mt."

February 1865 is the only month in recorded history not to have a full moon.

In the last 4,000 years, no new animals have been domesticated.

If the population of China walked past you, in single file, the line would never end because of the rate of reproduction.

If you are an average American, you will spend an average of 6 months waiting at red lights during your life.

It's impossible to sneeze with your eyes open.

Leonardo Da Vinci invented scissors.

Maine is the only state whose name is just one syllable.

No word in the English language rhymes with "month," "orange," "silver," or "purple."

Our eyes are always the same size from birth, but our nose and ears never stop growing.

Peanuts are one of the ingredients of dynamite.

Rubber bands last longer when refrigerated.

"Stewardesses" is the longest word typed with only the left hand and "lollipop" with the right.

The average person's left hand does 56 percent of the typing.

The cruise liner QE2 moves only six inches for each gallon of diesel that it burns.

The microwave was invented after a researcher walked by a radar tube and a chocolate bar melted in his pocket.

The sentence "The quick brown fox jumps over the lazy dog" uses every letter of the alphabet.

The winter of 1932 was so cold that Niagara Falls froze completely solid.

The words "racecar," "kayak," and "level" are the same whether they are read left to right or right to left (palindromes).

There are 293 ways to make change for a dollar.

There are more chickens than people in the world.

There are only four words in the English language that end in "dous": "tremendous," "horrendous," "stupendous," and "hazardous."

There are two words in the English language that have all five vowels in order: "abstemious" and "facetious."

There's no Betty Rubble in the Flintstones Chewable Vitamins.

Tigers have striped skin, not just striped fur.

"TYPEWRITER" is the longest word that can be made using the letters on only one row of the keyboard.

Women blink nearly twice as much as men.

An Incrdeible Discovery

Give each staff member the following (it's pretty amazing, isn't it?):

Aoccdrnig to a rscheearch at Cmabrigde Uinervtisy, it deosn't mttaer in waht oredr the ltteers in a wrod are, the olny iprmoetnt tihng is taht the frist and lsat ltteer be at the rghit pclae. The rset can be a total mses and you can sitll raed it wouthit porbelm. Tihs is bcuseae the huamn mnid deos not raed ervey lteter by istlef, but the wrod as a wlohe. Pettry amzanig huh?

Bumper Stumpers

This activity can be done individually, in teams, or as an entire group. Make either a worksheet featuring license plate images or create a similar PowerPoint presentation. Show the images one at a time, and have colleagues try to guess the messages. Start with a couple of easy ones, such as 4GIVEME (forgive me) or NOW8ING (no waiting), then introduce more complex ones.

1. IRIGHTI	10. SN2BMD
2. RUD14ME?	11. LVUBYBY
3. XQQSME	12. BHAPE
4. IM12XL	13. ICULOOKN
5. ULIV 1S	14. 2M8OS
6. H2OUUP2	15. 10SNE1
7. TI-3VOM	16. CALQL8
8. WYTXMAS	17. CME4AD8
9. L8RG8R	18. 4KIX

1. Right between the eyes 2. Are you 'da one for me? 3. Excuse me 4. I am one to excel 5. You live once 6. Water you up to 7. Move-It—as read from a rearview mirror 8. White Christmas 9. Later Gator 10. Soon to be MD (doctor) 11. Love you—Bye Bye 12. Be happy 13. I see you looking 14. Tomatoes 15. Tennis, anyone? 16. Calculate 17. See me for a date 18. For Kicks

GETTING TO KNOW EACH OTHER BETTER

60 Seconds

Select one or two people to participate in this activity each week. Ask rapid-fire questions for 60 seconds; the only rule is that staff members have to answer with the first thing they think of. Change the questions for each person so that no one can plan their answers in advance. Some possible questions are:

- What is your favorite movie?
- What is your favorite snack food?
- Name a movie you are ashamed to admit you liked.
- What is your favorite beverage?
- What is the strangest job you ever held?
- What is your favorite flavor of ice cream?
- What was the first concert you ever attended?
- What was your hardest subject in school?
- Other than education, what career would you choose?
- How long did you know your spouse before you got married?
- What is your favorite type of candy?
- Are you a meat or fish person?
- What is your favorite cologne?
- What was the first job you ever had?
- What is your nickname?
- What do you like to do for fun?
- Besides your family, what makes you smile?
- What do you do to relax?
- If a movie was made about our school, whom would you want to play you?
- What was the last big purchase you made?
- What is your favorite movie?
- What has been your biggest challenge?
- What was your childhood ambition?
- What is your favorite kind of music?

> Laughter is
> the shortest
> distance between
> two people.
>
> —*Victor Borge*

"Me" Boards

Give staff members mini-bulletin boards and instructions to fill their board with a collage of pictures that represent them, their family, friends, memories, events, hobbies, pets, etc. Voluntary staff members share their boards at the start of staff meetings throughout the year.

Staff-Led Meetings

Everyone is a leader and a learner, depending on the area. Allow those with the most knowledge (individuals or teams) in a particular subject to lead the best practices or book studies part of the meeting in that specific area.

Excellence Showcase

During staff meetings, showcase lesson plans that are exemplary. Individual staff members who are willing can present their own lesson plan(s), or the principal can present them. *(Samuel Smith School, Burlington, NJ)*

"Take-withs"

Educators love useful ideas. Add a "Take-with" category to the agenda. Staff members write up effective ideas, lesson plans, etc., and hand out copies of these "Take-withs" to colleagues at the meeting.

Are You This or That?

For this activity, you will need a room with enough space to move around in. Divide the staff members into two groups by the season in which they were born. The people with fall/winter birthdays go to one side of the room and those with spring/summer birthdays go to the opposite side.

Develop a series of topics, such as:

- Pool or lake
- McDonald's or Taco Bell
- Ford or Chevy
- Leno or Letterman
- Popcorn or candy at a movie
- Shower or bath
- Croutons or bacon bits
- Morning person or night owl
- Meat or fish

Depending on preferences, participants "vote with their feet" by going to the side of the room designated for either the first item (e.g., pool) or the opposite side for the second item (e.g., lake). There will be a lot of laughter as people go across the room or stay in place, and find out which of their colleagues share their preferences.

Variation:
Put up two signs—one that says "yes" and one with "no." Ask the following questions and learn more about the demographics of the staff.

Do you . . .

- Have a master's degree or above?
- Have a degree from an out-of-state school?
- Have children?
- Have parents living?
- Have parents living with you?
- Have grandchildren?
- Have a second job?
- Have more than three pets
- Etc.

Variation:
Using the same "yes" and "no" signs, read off an activity and staff members to go the side of the room that tells whether they have participated in each event.

Have you ever . . .

- Ridden on a plane?
- Swam in the ocean?
- Smoked cigarettes?
- Crashed a friend's car?
- Lost a job?
  - Gone on a blind date?
  - Skipped school?
  - Sang karaoke in a public place?
  - Paid for a meal with coins?
  - Made prank phone calls?
  - Caught a snowflake on your tongue?
  - Danced in the rain?
  - Sent a letter to Santa Claus?
    - Made a bonfire on a beach?
    - Showed up at the wrong wedding?
- Watched the sun rise with a special person?
- Laughed so hard you wet your pants?

 # PRINCIPAL-LED MEETINGS

Morning Meetings

Start each morning in the cafeteria with "Morning Meetings" attended by both students and staff members. It gets everyone starting the day in a focused, positive manner. If daily is hard to manage, then have "Monday Morning Meetings" to start the week off motivated and enthusiastic.

Staff Meeting Raffles

Obtain several donated prizes from local businesses such as bookstores, donut shops, restaurants, car wash companies, etc. Also visit flea markets and discount stores for inexpensive, playful items that are fun to win. You may also want to make up "no duty" coupons where the principal covers lunch or playground duty, or "My principal will wash my car" certificates. As faculty members enter the staff meeting, greet them with a smile, thank them for coming, and give each person a raffle ticket. At the end of the meeting, draw the winners. *(Moreau Hall Elementary School, Easton, MA)*

Turn Your Stress Around

We all know that there are some very stressful times of the year. To help turn the stress around, select seven people to take part in the following activity. Put one letter of the word "STRESSED" on large pieces of paper. Have the members hold the paper in front of them to spell out the word while you talk to the attendees about recent school events and say how much each person is appreciated. Tell them you want to "turn the stress around." The seven people then turn around, and on their backs are displayed the same letters in reverse order, spelling "DESSERTS." Bring in desserts for everyone to enjoy. It would be nice to have enough to take home a "doggie bag" too.

> Laughter is an instant vacation.
>
> —*Milton Berle*

Golden Box Giveaway

Another variation of the staff meeting raffle is to add an element of risk. Spray paint a large box a gold color. The raffle winner then has to make the decision as to whether he or she will keep this prize or select an unknown prize found inside the Golden Box. The prize in the Golden Box can be something of quality such as a gift certificate from a nice local store, dinner-for-two coupons—or it could be a "Wa Wa Waaaaa" gag gift. Such gag gifts could include a coffee mug displaying a picture of the principal, a toy rat, etc. The fun part comes when the staff tries to influence the winner to take the risk and choose what's in the Golden Box. Get ready to hear your colleagues chant "Box! Box! Box!" *(James Madison Elementary School, Sheboygan, WI)*

"FUN"damental Celebration

Throughout the year, recognize staff members for having fun on the job, cheering on colleagues, being caring individuals, and being optimistic.

Collect "awards" to be presented to four staff members at each staff meeting. Some examples of fun awards that relate to personal traits and contributions are:

- Having Fun—An elaborate party hat that says "Party Animal"
- Cheering on Others—Pom-Poms
- Caring—Hugging teddy bears
- Optimism—Artificial smiling flower in a pot

At the beginning of the year, have one person (possibly the principal) present each of the awards to four different people, explaining why each person was selected. Each recipient keeps his or her award until the next staff meeting, when they award them to new recipients and tell why the new recipients are deserving of the award. Individuals can receive the award multiple times as deserved.

Secret Mark

Several times a year, a "secret mark" is randomly placed on staff meeting or professional development agendas. The mark could reflect the season and appear as a snowflake, sunshine, etc. When it is announced, the staff members who have the mark on their agendas receive a prize (e.g., a school supply item). Note: Sales representatives can provide free samples that can be used as prizes. *(Nashville Primary School, Nashville, AR)*

The Good Stuff

Begin each meeting with "The Good Stuff." Staff members share something funny a student or parent did or said, a note or letter received, or a story to warm hearts and bring laughter. *(Cloverdale Elementary School, Moreno Valley, CA)*

Wishing Well

Place a wishing well, kiddie pool, or large bowl in the middle of the room. Give each staff member a penny. Each person has a turn to make a wish and share the wish with the group while tossing the penny (over the shoulder) into the well. The wishes could be for the new school year, particular students, personal goals, etc.

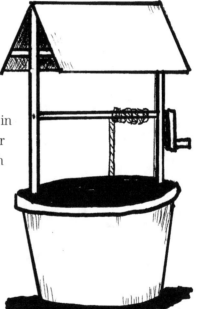

Chapter 6
Through the Day

FOOD AND FUN

Monday Munchies

Staff members divide into teams and each signs up for a designated Monday. On the selected Monday, group members bring in "munchies" to the staff lounge to share with their colleagues. These could include such items as Chex Mix, cookies, cupcakes, chips and dip, hot and cold appetizers, etc. Each group provides recipes for the items they prepare, to be compiled into a "Monday Munchies" cookbook.

Midweek Munchies

Have staff members sign up to host a "Midweek Munchies" day on Wednesday. On the designated day, the staff member brings in treats so that colleagues will visit his or her classroom. *(Samuel Smith School, Burlington, NJ)*

Signature Treat

Do you have a signature treat that people associate with you (e.g., Snickers candy bar, Tootsie Roll Pops, popcorn, etc.)? If so, capitalize on that by sharing your special treat with the staff. On the first day of school, put the treat in the staff mailboxes to welcome both new and old colleagues and to start the year off right. At the end of the marking period, do the same thing to thank staff members for their hard work. It's a simple way to show appreciation, and it's easy

for the recipient to know who it came from. *(John Tyson Elementary School, Springdale, AR)*

We Love You Tender

Send an e-card inviting staff members to an Elvis luncheon. The invitation can say something like "You are invited to an Elvis luncheon. Join us for fried peanut butter and banana sandwiches and chicken tenders." Decorate the area with Elvis memorabilia, play Elvis music, and have a guest appearance by an Elvis look-alike. Such fun! *(Reagan Elementary School, Rogers, AR)*

Parent-Teacher Conferences = Crock-Pot Day

"Crock-Pot Day" is a marvelous activity to incorporate into parent-teacher conference events. A week before the event, post a sign-up sheet asking staff members to volunteer to bring in a crock-pot item, salad, bread, paper product, or dessert. On parent-teacher conference days, staff members set up their crock-pots in the dining room early in the morning. By lunchtime, gourmet delights are ready. Because the crock-pots keep the food warm, staff members can go back to the dining room and grab another bite at their convenience. Who knows? This could be the start of a chili cook-off or perhaps a staff cookbook. *(Orchard Hill School, Skillman, NJ)*

Matt Driscoll, Principal of James Madison Elementary in Sheboygan, WI, tastes the bread he baked for his staff.

Homemade Bread—Mmm . . .

Early in the morning start making bread at school in bread machines placed throughout the campus. This will give staff members fresh bread to enjoy during their breaks, and students and staff love the "home-like" smell. *(James Madison Elementary School, Sheboygan, WI)*

"Cake" it Easy

Invite staff members to join together to "cake it easy" by having some cake and conversation at the end of the day.

LUNCH BUNCH

Lunch and Learn

Many work places have Lunch and Learn seminars during the noon hour. If the seminar lasts longer than the normal lunchtime, employees are to get their manager's approval to attend. The following flier announcing an upcoming seminar was sent to a group of employees:

Lunch and Learn Seminar

Who's Controlling Your Life?

(Get your manager's permission before attending.)

Gourmet PB&J Day

Have a gourmet peanut butter and jelly sandwich day. Ask various people to bring in the staples of bread, peanut butter (crunch and smooth) and jelly. Ask other staff members to bring in an additional item to experiment with in adding to the creation (e.g. apple slices, bananas, cucumbers, whole peanuts, etc.)

"Guess Who?" Potluck Lunch

Have interested staff members prepare a dish for a staff potluck. Label each food item with a number and the name of the dish. Give each person a list of the food items and participating staff members' names. Ask staff members to match the food item with the names. The people with the highest number of correct answers get to be first in line for dessert.

"Special" Potluck Meal

Often people have a favorite family recipe or a signature dish that has a story or memory associated with it. Ask staff members to prepare their dishes and then share the story that accompanies the dish.

Themed Luncheons

Have a themed staff luncheon once a month. Staff members sign up to bring in the fixings. *(McCluer Senior High School, Florissant, MO)* Examples of themes include:

It's Getting Hot in Here – chili and salads
Spud Day – baked potato luncheon
Crazy Spaghetti Luncheon – with lots of garlic bread
Thank Goodness it's the Holiday – turkey luncheon

Soup-er Monday

Each Monday staff members take turns in preparing and sharing their favorite soups with their colleagues. Collect the recipes to create a staff cookbook.

Order Out Day

Once a month, hold a drawing with all staff member's names entered. The winner receives a lunch delivered from a local restaurant.

Meatloaf Mondays

Everyone seems to have a favorite meatloaf recipe. Ask staff members to sign up for a Monday lunch where they prepare and bring in meatloaves. If there are many participants, divide them into groups and have "Meatloaf Mondays" for several weeks or months. Provide bread and condiments to make sandwiches. Provide copies of the recipes or create a staff cookbook.

Salsa Day

Have staff members prepare or purchase their favorite salsas. Bring in tortilla chips and label the salsas mild, medium, and HOT!

This is Our Country

Staff members often hail from many different states. In this situation, have the staff divide up by the state or part of the country where they grew up.

On Mondays, plan a themed lunch around a designated state food. Each group signs up to provide food that represents their part of the country. Keep the preparations simple but fun. The groups may want to select a name for the day such as "Aloha Monday." The lounge can be decorated with items consistent with the theme; music can also add ambiance. Participants can wear clothes that represent the universities or states as well.

Not every state has an official food, so you can offer popular foods commonly found in that part of the country. Suggestions for each state are listed.

Alabama	Peanut and pecan pie
Alaska	Salmon and halibut
Arizona	Prickly pear cactus
Arkansas	Barbeque ribs
California	Avocado
Colorado	Rainbow trout
Connecticut	Nutmeg
Delaware	Crab puffs
District of Columbia	Senate bean soup
Florida	Oranges and Key lime pie
Georgia	Peaches, pecans, Vidalia onions, and grits
Hawaii	Pineapple
Idaho	Potato
Illinois	The official state snack food is popcorn (2004)
Indiana	Pork and pork & beans
Iowa	Corn
Kansas	Wheat
Kentucky	Is bourbon a food? Derby pie
Louisiana	Gumbo is the official state cuisine (2004) and beignet is the official state donut (1986); red beans and rice, pralines, and jambalaya
Maine	Blueberries and lobster
Maryland	Crab cakes
Massachusetts	Corn muffin is the official muffin (1986) and chocolate cookie is the official cookie (1997); clam chowder
Michigan	Cherry and pastries in the Upper Peninsula
Minnesota	Blueberry muffin is the official muffin (1988); wild rice, walleye, and SPAM
Mississippi	Catfish, mud pie, pecan pie, sweet potato pie, shrimp

Missouri	Ozark pudding and crayfish
Montana	Buffalo burgers
Nebraska	Beef and watermelon
Nevada	Trout
New Hampshire	Corn chowder
New Jersey	Campbell's tomato soup, saltwater taffy, and cranberries
New Mexico	Chili and biscochito (sugar cookies)
New York	Bagel, pizza, Waldorf salad, and Jell-O
North Carolina	Sweet potato
North Dakota	Perch and Cream of Wheat
Ohio	Tomato juice is the state beverage (1965)
Oklahoma	Chicken-fried steak
Oregon	Hazelnuts, blackberries, marionberries, and peppermint
Pennsylvania	Chocolate chip cookie is the official cookie (2003) and Lebanon bologna
Rhode Island	Johnnycakes (corn bread)
South Carolina	Shrimp and rice
South Dakota	Fry bread is the official bread (2005)
Tennessee	Stack cake
Texas	Chili is the official state dish (1977) and the official state snack is tortilla chips and salsa (2003)
Utah	Honey
Vermont	The apple is the state pie (1999), maple syrup
Virginia	Ham and peanuts
Washington	Apples and Dungeness crab
West Virginia	Apple butter and Golden Delicious apples
Wisconsin	Cheese
Wyoming	Buffalo and jerky

If the foods listed are not conducive to a lunch environment, then you could offer snacks for a staff meeting instead. Or you could have a theme that represents a specific state (e.g., the Cubs and the White Sox baseball teams for Illinois). Plan a "Take Me Out to the Ball Game" lunch with hot dogs, peanuts, and popcorn.

This is Our World

Have the same type of activity described in *This is Our Country,* but serve food from different countries. If you have an internationally diverse staff, have them prepare foods from their countries. Otherwise, have teams sign up to serve foods found in countries such as Italy, Greece, France, and Mexico. Include the country's flag, music, posters, etc., to help make the meal more festive.

JUST FOR THE FUN OF IT

Booster Baskets

Participation in the "booster basket" activity allows staff members to take part in a traveling basket filled with their favorite goodies throughout the year. Those who want to participate complete a questionnaire regarding their favorite things; the principal keeps the information.

One person, usually the principal, starts the activity by purchasing a wicker-type basket and selects the name of the first recipient. The basket is filled with that individual's favorite goodies and is delivered to him or her. Within a week, that person draws the name of the next recipient and fills the basket with a new set of treats. Staff members can identify themselves when they deliver the basket, but many choose to keep their colleagues in suspense. This is a great way to boost spirits and make someone's day! *(Northland Pines Middle School, Eagle River, WI)*

Name _____
What is your favorite type of:
Soda/Juice _____
Coffee/Tea _____
Book or Magazine _____
Sandwich _____
Flower _____
Scent/Smell _____
Color _____
Hobbies/Collectibles _____
Additional Information _____

Snow Day Contest

Post a winter calendar where staff members congregate. Ask each person to pick a day they think will be the first Snow Day. Allow three names per day. The first person's name on a given day receives the first place prize; the second name, second place prize, etc. Designate a blank square on the calendar for the selection of "No Snow Day." If the last selected calendar day passes before there is a Snow Day, the people who signed up for the "No Snow Day" become the winners. To add to the suspense, cross off each day that goes by without a Snow Day. *(Debra Macklin, Quincy, MI)* The winners receive prizes such as:

First Place: An adjustable snow shovel with a matching ice scraper and brush

Second Place: Purple flying saucer and hand warmers

Third Place: A gallon of windshield washer fluid and bag of Ice Melt

E-mail Trivia Challenge

E-mail staff members a trivia question each morning. The first five winners get to select a prize from the Trivia Box, which consists of goodies from the Oriental Trading Company. On Monday, 10 winners are selected. *(Debra Macklin, Quincy, MI)* A few starters are:

1. What is the longest word you can spell without repeating a letter?
2. What is the longest word with just one vowel?
3. What is the only English word with a triple letter?
4. What is the word with the longest definition in most dictionaries?
5. What is the shortest "ology" (study of) word?
6. What is the only word in which an "f" is pronounced like a "v"?

1. uncopyrightable; 2. strengths; 3. goddesship; 4. set; 5. oology, the study of eggs; 6. of

Half Way There

Throw a "Half Way There" party at the start of the second semester. Everything about the celebration is done in halves—cut all of the food in half and serve half cups of beverages. Cut the agenda or a message into half and instruct the staff members to pair up with the person who has the other half so they can read the full text. Distribute cards with the names of half a "dynamic duo" and have participants find their partners (e.g., Abbott and Costello, Batman and Robin, Sonny and Cher, Cheech and Chong, The Lone Ranger and Tonto, etc.). Ask restaurants or retail stores to donate coupons for half off a meal or item, or a "buy one, get one free" offer. Hold a drawing for prizes half way through the party.

Paycheck Poker

Before checks are given out on paydays, staff members who want to participate can contribute a dollar to play Paycheck Poker. Roll dice to determine that week's "wild number." Using the numerals on the serial number on the paycheck, the person with the best poker "hand" wins half the money collected. The remaining money is set aside for whatever the staff decides (e.g., a party at the end of the year, something for the school, etc.). *(Quincy Community Schools, Quincy, MI)* The best poker hands (in order) are:

Four of a Kind   Four of the same numbers (e.g., 5555 would beat 4444)

Full House   Three of the same number and two of another number (e.g., 99944 would beat 88899 because 9 is higher)

Straight   Five numbers in a sequence (e.g., 98765 or 23456)

Three of a Kind   Three of the same number

Two Pairs   A pair is two of the same numbers. You need two pairs. (e.g., 9922 or 8899. The winner would be 9922)

One Pair   Two of the same number

Example of a check number 98777329. The holder has a full house with 77799. If 3 were the wild number, the holder would have 7777. In case of a tie, a natural (no use of a wild number) wins.

Draw Down

Before a holiday or vacation, have a Draw Down. Staff members who want to participate contribute one dollar per chance at winning and put their names on a corresponding number of entry slips (e.g., 3 chances for $3). When the money is collected, divide the number of chances by the number of days you want to run the event. For instance, if 25 chances are purchased and you want to run the event for five days, you would draw five names per day.

Divide the number of work hours by the number of draws so the drawings are spaced throughout the day (e.g., 5 names selected each day for an 8-hour day; drawings would occur each 1.5 hours).

Put the entry slips into a container and mix them up. Each day, have various volunteers draw one name at a time. The first name drawn each day gets his or her dollar back. The other names drawn during the remainder of the day are eliminated from the game unless they bought multiple chances.

E-mail the winner's name to all participants and then in a series of e-mails throughout the day, identify one person at a time whose name has been eliminated. You can add fun remarks for the winner and nonwinners (e.g., "John Smith, I hope you weren't planning to eat off the dollar menu at McDonald's today because you're out! Sorry.").

At the end of the game period, the last two names remaining split the proceeds. You could divide them 60/40, or you could allocate half for charity or a staff event and let the winners split the remaining proceeds. Your choice.

Variation: Second Chance Drawing—Each time a name is eliminated, the person has an opportunity to put fifty cents into a new drawing. At the end of the time period, one name is drawn and receives the money collected. (*Debra Macklin, Quincy, MI*)

Work is either fun or drudgery. It depends on your attitude. I like fun.

—*Colleen C. Barrett*

Live and work, but do not forget to play, to have fun in life, and really enjoy it.

—*Eileen Caddy*

Bad Hair Day

Staff members come to work with their own creative version of a Bad Hair Day. Students can also participate.

Other days that can be planned are Tropical Day, Comfort Day, Fake Injury Day, etc.

Smile Center

Make a large smiley face out of yellow poster board and label it "Smile Center." Put rectangular-shaped poster board underneath it. Periodically add jokes, funny stories, cartoons, etc. When you take down the old items, put them into a notebook titled "Smile File." You can also add interesting Web sites, helpful hints, quotes, etc., to the notebook. This gives substitute teachers and other staff members something to look at and smile. *(Debra Macklin, Quincy, MI)*

Chocolate Day

Designate a Chocolate Day for the staff. Staff members or administrators can provide chocolate goodies (e.g., hot chocolate, candy, cookies, ice cream, chocolate-covered cherries, etc.) in the faculty lounge.

And keep a supply of chocolate at your desk. You'll be happy to see how many of your colleagues stop by to chat. *(Berkley Street School, New Milford, NJ and Stackhouse School, Pemberton, NJ)*

Stop Everything—Dance!

Select high-energy music such as *Mustang Sally* (by Wilson Pickett), *We Are Family* (by The Pointer Sisters), or *I Feel Good* (by James Brown). Play the music at a staff meeting and have members choose the song they find most energizing, invigorating, stress relieving. Tell them that when they hear this music, they should stop what they're doing, go to a designated location, and join together in a dance. Most groups form double lines (such as with the Stroll), with opposite partners moving down the center of the line together. No one says anything—people should just dance, smile, snap their fingers, sing, and enjoy themselves. Visitors can join in and have fun, too. When the music is over, staff members return to work with a renewed attitude of joy and fun.

Concerts in the School

Staff members bring in their favorite CD to play over the PA system after the students leave for the day.

Decorate Their Shoes

Ask staff members to each bring in a pair of old shoes. Provide a workstation that has decorative items such as ribbon, yarn, sequins, glue, feathers, etc. Staff members can also bring in decorative items of their choice. Either label the shoes with the owner's name so they can be customized, or let them be anonymous (it's sometimes a surprise to find out who the owner is). Each staff member selects a pair of shoes and decorates that pair. The decorators and owners match up on a specific day, and the owners wear their decorated shoes to school.

An Educator Is . . .

Give each staff member the sentence starter An educator is _____. Have them give one-word adjectives to finish the sentence. Write down the silly, fun, and serious responses and distribute the list to staff members.

Mind Over Monday

On the first Monday of every month have a "Mind Over Monday" gathering. Staff members meet before students arrive and enjoy foods such as fruit, sausage biscuits, etc., while talking about everything except school. *(Blountsville Elementary School, Blountsville, AL)*

No "NO" Monday

Designate one Monday as a day that staff members may not use the word "no." Explain that they have to find other ways to express their feelings. If "no" is spoken, a piece of masking tape is placed on the staff member's shirt. The person with the least number of pieces of tape at the end of the day gets a prize.

Don't Eat Lunch with Grouches

Supply the staff lounge with water pistols and Nerf balls. Whenever someone is negative, staff members are free to use these toys to give their colleague an "attitude adjustment."

Flying Animals

Keep a basket of stuffed, plush animals in the lounge. Tell staff members that they can throw around these toys when they are frustrated—or when they just want to have fun. And remember to keep some in your work area, too; you might just need them sometime. *(Debra Macklin, Quincy, MI)*

Good Days Jar

Designate a jar as the staff's *Good Day Jar*. When a staff member has a particularly good day or solves a difficulty in a positive manner, he or she puts a marble in the jar and shares the events with the staff. When the jar is full, have a "Good Day" celebration.

Star-Studded Staff

Designate a week as a "star studded" week. Introduce it at the staff meeting by throwing gold stars in the air. Staff members will most likely be confused, but explain that throughout the week stars will appear everywhere. When they find a star, they should write their name on it and put it in the designated basket in the office. Throughout the day, put stars in the restrooms, lounge, copy room, hallways, cafeteria, etc., places the staff frequents. Drop some in the classrooms when doing a walkthrough or at the bus stations when students are departing. Warning: Staff members may be spotted running in all directions, following you closely, and looking like children young at heart. At the end of each day, raffle off prizes (to be paid for with stars, of course). Prizes include plants from the floriculture program, items from the supply closet, or other donated items. *(Ross Elementary School, Milford, DE)*

"Stress Down" Day

Transfer the staff lounge into a spa. Place small fountains in the room to provide soft, tranquil sounds. Dim the lights, scent the room with potpourri, and play relaxing music. Have massage therapists or students from massage schools give chair massages to staff members during their planning periods or breaks. Or have manicurists giving hand massages complete with warming lotion. *(West Middleton Elementary School, Verona, WI)*

Poetry Readings

Create an "alternative environment" with candles and the music of John Lennon. Staff members read their favorite poems—each full of meaning and messages. Original poetry is really valued. You'll learn a great deal about colleagues through their selection.

Fine for Fun

Late?? Late getting the lesson plans in? Late with your grades? Late for the staff meeting? Determine a lateness fine: $1 to $5. Each time someone is late, assess the "staff fine." The money can be used for a staff-related event.

Hobby Showcase

Life outside of work? Many staff members have very rich lives that aren't always known to their colleagues. Invite staff members to bring in an item that represents one of their hobbies or interests (e.g., fishing pole, miniature sewing machine, jewelry, gardening gloves, music, etc.) and tell the group what the item represents and means to them. You can also make it challenging by asking staff members to match the item with the person.

Human Sundae

Set a goal with staff members for an achievement that is both challenging and rewarding (e.g., increased test scores, revising the curriculum, etc.). Tell them that the reward for reaching the goal is "a human sundae." An administrator or staff member agrees to be a human sundae created by the staff. Lay plastic on the floor and wear old clothes. Supply the staff with whip cream cans, chocolate syrup, nuts, and a cherry for the top. You might want to have the fixings for ice cream sundaes for all the staff as well. Be sure to take plenty of photos. (This could also be used as a student incentive to read books, score well on standardized tests, improve attendance, etc.)

Tickets Drawing

Parents or community members often have tickets to cultural or sporting events that they can't use. Ask them to make these tickets available to staff members. Hold a drawing for each set of tickets.

Hats Off to You

Ask staff members to take pictures of themselves wearing a hat and then post the photos on the computer or in the lounge. Throughout the week, staff members vote for the winners of categories such as "Most Creative," "Funniest," "Prettiest," etc. On the last day, have all participants wear their respective hats to school. After the students leave, gather the staff together and announce the winners. Serve hat-shaped cake, and then give out the prizes to the winners

Marc and Jeff Hodges

Jeff Hodges

Gerry Martin

Diane Hodges

Catch Them Off Guard

Do fun, silly things that catch staff members off guard.
For example:

- Put a sign on the photocopier indicating that it has been retrofitted and is now voice activated. Instruct them to place their original on the glass and speak the instructions to the machine. Catch them talking to the machine.
- Dress up like a flight attendant and either greet staff members at the door in the morning with a tiny bag of pretzels, or say "Ba-bye" at the end of the day.

Retro Play Day

Many staff members grew up before computer/video games, television, and iPods. Games at that time were very basic. Host a "Retro Play Day" in which the games played are marbles, jacks, pick up sticks, hop scotch, Cootie, jump rope—nothing that needs batteries. Warning: Instructions might be necessary for the younger folks!

TEAM CHALLENGES

Crossword Puzzle Challenges

Enlarge a crossword puzzle and post multiple copies on a wall where people congregate during the workday (e.g., faculty lounge). Divide the staff into small groups (mix people who don't normally work together or who are in different subject/grade levels) and assign each group to a puzzle. Allow time before each staff meeting for the groups to work on the puzzle. Award a prize to the group that completes the puzzle first.

Variation: Have each team work on a different crossword puzzle. The event is not competitive, but allows staff members to work together on a project and get to know each other better.

Staff Members: Start Your Shopping Carts!

Version #1: 10 in 10 — You'll need to do this activity away from the school grounds (e.g., a large store such as a Wal-Mart or K-Mart), and permission from the store is recommended. Divide the staff into groups and give each team a shopping cart. Each team selects a captain. The captains have 10 minutes to put 10 items into their shopping cart. The carts are then turned over to members of the opposing teams, who have to figure out where the items belong in the store and return them to those locations. The first team back to the check-out counters with an empty cart is the winner. To keep things honest, have a member of the opposing team accompany the shopping cart.

Version #2: A to Z — Divide the staff into teams. The first team to find an item and place it into the cart for every letter in the alphabet wins. Remember: ALL items must be put back in the correct locations on the shelves!

Beautify the School

Divide the staff into teams, pairing people who don't usually have daily interaction (e.g., people working with different grade levels, special programs, etc.) and give each group $250. The groups identify an area of the school to beautify and then complete the task. Examples are decorating restrooms, improving landscaping, or sprucing up the faculty lounge, hallways, or cafeteria. *(Weimar Elementary School, Weimar, TX)*

Kickball Challenge

Plan a kickball game in which staff members challenge each other and the students cheer them on. Field Days can be fun for everyone! *(Central School, Wall Township, NJ)*

Crazy Triathlon

Organize a triathlon of three highly competitive, energy-zapping, physically challenging events such as bowling, shuffleboard, pool, hopscotch, tetherball, jacks, ring toss, or croquet.

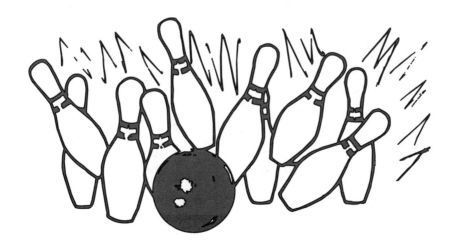

FOR THE HEALTH OF IT!

Big Fat Loser

At the start of the new year, voluntary staff members who want to lose weight weigh in on the same day. A chart is made for each person to record their progress, and all records are on the honor system. Each week, staff members each put $1.00 into a weight-loss pot and record their gain or loss for the week. If there is a weight gain, an additional $1.00 is put into the pot for each pound or 25 cents for each quarter pound gained. On the Friday before Spring Break, the person who lost the most weight receives the money in the pot. *(Debra Macklin, Quincy, MI)*

100 Pounds Lighter

Staff set a goal to lose a cumulative 100 pounds (participation is voluntary and anonymous). Post a chart in the faculty lounge on which participants mark each pound lost (but if they lose weight and then gain it back, they cannot re-enter the pounds). When the goal of 100 pounds is reached, give anonymous surprise prizes. To assist in this process, form exercise groups to walk after work in the halls or outside. *(Ashgrove School, Riverton, WY)*

Garlic—It's Good for You!

Place a garlic bulb in each staff member's mailbox along with tips about the healthy qualities it possesses. (It makes for terrific laughter and conversation.) *(Happy Thought Elementary School, Selkirk, Manitoba, Canada)*

Walk to Health

Divide staff members who want to participate into walking groups. Each week the teams record the number of miles they walk and report their success to the other groups. At the end of nine weeks, hold a recognition celebration and give fun awards such as walking socks, pedometers, certificates of participation, etc., to the walkers. Give an award to the individual and the group who recorded the most miles walked. *(Upton Elementary School, Upton, WY)*

Chapter 7
To the End

END OF THE SCHOOL YEAR

1:1 Meeting

At the end of the school year, the principal
schedules an individual 10–15 minute
meeting with each staff member
(complete with snacks). Praise,
kudos, compliments are given for
specific actions that the staff member
performed sometime during the year.
*(Grandview Intermediate School
District, Grandview, TX)*

Dare to Dream

At the end of the school year, give
each staff person a questionnaire
asking what they would like to make
their job easier and for them to be effective the next year.
Staff members can wish for supplies, books, decorations, etc.
The principal then tries to have 2–3 of these items for them
when the school year starts. *(Grandview Elementary
School, Grandview, TX)*

END OF THE YEAR TREATS

As the end of the year approaches, prepare motivational,
appreciative treats for staff members. Put one in their

mailboxes each day. They will look forward to their daily surprise.

Cheez-It Crackers

Attach the following to a small bag of Cheez-It crackers:

C *heers!* **I** *ncredible!*

H *allelujah!* **T** *errific!*

E *xcellent!*

E *xuberation!*

Z *uper!*

(These are words overheard in the cafeteria as students were discussing the staff members—honest)

Certificate to Perkins Restaurant

Attach the following to the certificate:

Pause the pandemonium! Picky practitioners primarily prefer Perkins (particularly the pastries) to positively pack on pounds prior to partying and playing.

Apple Juice

Attach to a small bottle of apple juice:

You are the apple of our students' eyes, "juice" because you care!

Little Debbie Cake with Nuts

Attach to the cake:

Here is a little something sweet from your good friend, Little Debbie, to help you through the last few "nutty" days of the school year.

Small Package of Oreo Cookies

Attach to the cookies:

Oreo Cookies. Enough said.

Small Cup of Pudding

Attach to the pudding:

All of the ♡ you're "pudding" into your work shows in our students' smiles. Thank you!

Small Package of Pringles Potato Chips

Attach to potato chips:

You have made a big difference this year by "chipping" in as part of our team. Thank you!

Bite-Sized Snickers Candy Bar

Attach to candy bar and also place small baskets of Snickers in various places around the office:

Here's a Snickers
There's a Snickers
Everywhere there are Snickers

Small Bottle of Tropicana Orange Juice

Attach to the orange juice:

Knock, knock.
Who's there?
Orange.
Orange who?
Orange you glad the year is almost over?

Small Neon-Colored Notepads

Attach to the notepads:

We "note"iced all of your hard work this year. Thanks!

Hollow Chocolate Egg

Attach to the candy egg:

As you are "scrambling" to do 10 things
at once, please know that your
"egg"cellent work is appreciated.

(Phineas Davis Elementary School, York, PA)

End-of-the-Year Celebration

I had the opportunity to be the speaker at the Cincinnati College Preparatory Academy's "Tribute to Teachers" event. It is an inner-city charter elementary school with 535 students that is truly amazing. The event included a men's chorus, motivational and inspirational guest speakers, luncheon, media presentation summary of the year's activities, and recognition of staff members. Gorgeous awards and monetary recognitions were given for academic achievement, perfect attendance, and going the extra mile. The Extra Mile award was a bronze tennis shoe with "Extra Mile Award" engraved on it. Awards were also given for the Staff Member of the Year, Rookie of the Year, Teacher of the Year, and Teacher Distinction Awards.

Each staff member received a gold medal resembling those given to Olympic champions. A positive statement about the recipient was engraved on the back of that person's medal. Each staff member received a gift bag with such items as a gift certificate for an athletic shoe store or bookstore—very nice and useful items.

In a previous year the gift bag had been filled with beach accessories for summer. It was a truly exhilarating and enjoyable experience for all, and an amazing way to end the year.

End-of-the-Year Awards

There are many additional end of the year awards that can be given to staff members based on accomplishments or character traits.

After Hours Award

The staff member most likely to be at work after hours

School Spirit Award

The person who shows the most school spirit

Hostess with the Mostest Award

The person who had the most parents at Open House or who does nice things for colleagues

Cheerleader Award

Pom-poms given to the person who is always cheering on new initiatives and ideas

Adhesive Award

A large bottle of glue for the person who held everyone together

Fire Extinguisher Award

The person who put out the most fires during the school year

On the Bus ("You're either on the bus or off the bus")

The person who shows the most dedication to the school

Most Likely to OD on Coffee

The biggest coffee lover among the staff

Biggest Blunder Award

The person who made the biggest faux pas—and laughed about it

Paper Plate Awards Day

Plan this event to be held during the last inservice day or the last day of the year. Announce to the staff that fun awards will be given and the nominations started. The awards are decorated paper plates. The person who nominates a staff member is responsible for making the award. These are fun, lighthearted awards. Some examples might be "Post-it Note Award." The paper plate is decorated with all different shapes and colors of Post-it Notes because the teacher who is the recipient loves Post-it notes and can cram more information into one little note than anyone has ever seen. Another might be the "Where's BJ? Award" in which the plate is decorated like *Where's Waldo.* The award is given to a staff member who is never where he or she is supposed to be.

Have the emcee dress up in formal attire and announce the awards just like they do for the Emmys. The recipients get to say their thank-yous to all of those "who made it possible." It's a great way to end the year—loads of FUN!
(Fort Cherry Elementary Center, McDonald, PA)

Section III

Celebrating with Coworkers

Celebrate the happiness that friends are always giving,
make every day a holiday and celebrate just living!
—Amanda Bradley

Chapter 8
Caring and Sharing

BIRTHDAYS

Birthday Banners

Each month make and hang banners with the names and birth dates of staff members who are celebrating birthdays that month. On the specific day, include a birthday greeting to the staff person during the school's daily announcements. *(Petersburg Elementary School, Petersburg, TX)*

Birthday Signs

Make a sign that can be attached to a classroom door, cubicle, or other workstation to show who's having a special day—a birthday! Add some balloons for an extra treat.

A Month of Birthdays

Once a month, staff members bring in food and a huge birthday cake to celebrate those with birthdays that month. The staff lounge is decorated with the names of the "birthday celebrities" and other fun things that represent them. Staff members can snack all day and shower the birthday folks with good wishes and a lot of praise.

"Favorite" Birthday

At the start of the school year (or when new staff members are hired), ask each person to fill out a "Favorites List." On it they designate their favorite soda, candy, cookie, tea, gum, salty treat, snack food, music, etc. On each person's birthday, hand deliver a birthday bag that has some of those favorite things. *(Grandview Elementary School, Grandview, TX)*

Birthday Wreaths

Make a birthday wreath that is placed at the staff member's workstation on his or her birthday. If there are multiple birthdays on the same date, then the wreath can be rotated from door to door. Summer birthdays are celebrated in the fall or spring.

> May you live all the days of your life.
>
> —Jonathan Swift

Cross-Section Day

For the person's birthday, a cross-section of events are planned with a variety of staff members. For example, some may meet for a birthday breakfast, and then another group goes with the birthday person for a bike ride, and then another group goes to a movie together. This gives the birthday person a cross-section of things he or she loves to do.

E-cards

The Internet has made it simple, convenient, and inexpensive to send electronic greeting cards. Sites such as Hallmark.com and cloudeight.com make remembering and celebrating staff members' birthdays a fun event.

There *IS* Such a Thing as a Free Lunch!

Staff members receive a card and a coupon redeemable for a free lunch on their birthday. Who said there is no such thing as a free lunch? *(Miller Grove School, Cumby, TX)*

Free Lunch Coupon!

This coupon is redemable for one FREE lunch on your birthday.

Name _____

Restaurant _____

Date _____

Watch it Grow

Each staff member receives a live tree as a birthday gift and colleagues help plant it on school grounds. This allows staff members to have their own trees to take care of and watch grow through the years.

Birthday Store

Purchase fun items from the dollar stores and place them in the "Birthday Store." When staff members have a birthday, they are invited to "shop" for an item of their choice.

Make it a Surprise

Celebrate staff members' birthdays in creative ways—ways they would not be expecting. For example, stage a "problem" that requires the principal's attention. When the principal goes to attend to the issue, the children are lined up in the hall and sing "Happy Birthday" as soon as he or she appears. *(Trinity Temple Academy, Hillside, NJ)*

Kindnesses for the Day

Arrange for people to take very good care of the birthday person for the day. For example, have hot coffee and a snack waiting when he or she arrives, have a treat available for their planning period. You can also offer assistance to ensure the birthday person can leave work on time (or even earlier), warm up the car at the end of the day and drive it to the door, etc.

Gifts of Time

Version #1: When staff members have a birthday, give the "gift of time" by doing their job for 30 to 45 minutes. This applies to all staff—teaching, clerical, custodial, etc. It gives the birthday guy or gal a bit of personal time, and the staff member filling in learns something about the other person's job. For summer birthdays, find a mutually agreeable time to show appreciation with these gifts of time. *(Copeland Intermediate School District, Huffman, TX)*

Version #2: You could also give the person a "Gifts of Time" coupon book in which various staff members volunteer to do something useful for the birthday person. Ideas include helping put up storm windows, raking leaves in the birthday person's yard, or taking care of his or her kids for a weekend night. No monetary gifts are given.

Quote Book

Make a quote book or card of your favorite birthday quotes. Here are a few starters:

Happy Birthday Quotes for Janey

Don't just count the years, make your years count.

~Ernest Meyers

Youth is the gift of nature, but age is a work of art.

~ Garson Kanin

Why is a birthday cake the only food you can blow on and spit on and everybody rushes to get a piece?

~Bobby Kelton

Everyone is the age of their heart.

~Guatemalan proverb

You are never too old to set another goal or to dream a new dream.

~ Les Brown

Age is a number and mine is unlisted.

~Anonymous

If wrinkles are to be written upon our brows, let them not be written upon the heart. The spirit should never grow old.

~ James A. Garfield

A true friend remembers your birthday but not your age.

~ Unknown

The first hundred years are the hardest.

~ Wilson Mizner

Words of Praise

Hide words of praise, upbeat birthday quotes, or fun jokes around the room—on the person's desk, computer keyboard or monitor, in books, cupboards, file folders, etc. You might want to start them with *"You are special because . . . _____."* If you know the person's age, you could hide one for every year of his or her age (e.g., 40 affirmations for the person turning 40).

Theme Birthdays

Plan celebrations that correspond to the recipients' passions. For example, if the person loves the beach, decorate with beach towels, make palm trees out of construction paper,

> Birthdays are good for you. Statistics show that the people who have the most live the longest.
>
> *—Larry Lorenzoni*

and put up posters of beach scenes. Add some tropical music and punch with those cute little umbrellas. Have everyone dress in beach clothes (e.g., shorts, sandals,

etc.). Or, perhaps the person loves baseball. Make the location into the "field of dreams" or a ballpark. Serve refreshments from a concession stand or have a couple of staff members act as vendors who yell "hot dogs!" The perfect foods include hot dogs, popcorn, soda, nachos, peanuts, etc.

To add to the fun, you can have a pitching contest. Set up a pyramid of soda cans, draw a line to represent the pitcher's mound, and then have staff members try to knock over as many cans as possible with each pitch.

Birthday Present Activity

You will need a pair of gloves, a hat, a die, a present wrapped in several layers of newspaper and multiple boxes, and separate birthday gifts for all participants.

Wrap a gift in multiple boxes and with many layers of newspaper. At a staff gathering, ask all of those with birthdays that month to form a circle. Put the gloves, hat, and wrapped box in the center of the circle. Give the die to one birthday person to roll. The die is passed to the next person until a "6" is rolled. When it is, the person gives the die to the next person, then runs into the circle, puts on the gloves and hat, and begins unwrapping the package. That person has to move quickly because the next one who rolls a

"6" takes the hat off the person in the center (who must also give the gloves to the new person, and then go back to the edge of the circle). The game continues until the package is completely unwrapped. The person who finally unwraps the gift gets to keep it. Give each birthday person a gift that is different from the one used in the game.

 # RETIREMENT

Retirement Shower

Showers are typically given for staff members who get married or have a baby. Why not give a retirement shower for the staff members who are entering the next chapter of their lives?

Happy Retirement, Eddie!

Join us for a Retirement Shower for . . . Eddie Schwartz

Date ___May 21___

Time ___from 3:00 to 4:00___

Place ___the Cafeteria___

You can now catch up on those naps, take long lunch breaks, have time for gardening, grandchildren, cooking, reading, movies, and just enjoying quiet time at home.

Now as you retire, take time to be with family, have fun, keep active, make new friends (but don't forget the old!), kick up your heels, and throw away the clock!

Two weeks before the event, send invitations (such as the one shown) to staff members.

Decorate the room and have each staff member bring a gift that will be useful in retirement. Gifts could include books, gardening tools or hat, movie tickets, handmade gifts, gift certificates—personalized gifts that pertain to "life after education." *(Christoval High School, Christoval, TX)*

Handyman Party

Have a retirement party with a "Handyman" theme. Guests bring gift items that need repair (e.g., VCR, watch, etc.). This will give him plenty to do in his spare time.

No More Wake-ups

Give the retiree an alarm clock or watch with no hands, or wrap a clock in a bag and have the retiree smash it—because there's no need for wake-ups in retirement.

> Retirement at sixty-five is ridiculous. When I was sixty-five I still had pimples."
>
> —*George Burns*

Gag Retirement Party Gift Baskets

Make gift baskets for all retirees. Purchase large baskets and weave colored ribbon around them, and make a bow in the front. Fill them with gag goodies and attach explanations for each item. Keep in mind that some items are gender specific. Most of the gifts can be bought at Big Lots or The Dollar Store, and sample- or travel-size products also work great. The gift basket you put together might include:

DEPENDS	For those times when a panty liner just isn't enough!
PANTY LINERS	For those sneaky, unexpected sneezes!
PREPARATION H	For those days when you need a "soft touch." *(To save money, purchase a box of individually wrapped wipes and divide them among the retirees.)*
MAGNIFYING MIRROR & TWEEZERS	For those pesky "whiskers" that just pop up!
NOTEPAD & CRAYON	For those times when you're not sure what you should be doing. *(Tape a crayon to a small notepad.)*
RAIN BONNET	No retired gal would be caught without one!
BIB	For those crumbs that always land on the "top shelf."
CHARMIN TO GO	For when you "gotta go now," and the closest place is a cornfield.
PAIN PATCHES	Too much golf, gardening, lying around? Just slap one on!
MANICURE SET	You'll have plenty of time to do those nails now!
CANDY BAR	Eat dessert first!
CALCIUM CHEWS	Gotta keep them old bones strong!

PRUNES	It's important to stay "regular" at your age!
ENEMA	When prunes just aren't enough.
ANTIDIARRHEA MEDICATION	When the prunes and enema work too well!
TISSUES	Everyone knows that an elderly lady will have some in her purse.
PILL SORTER	We KNOW you're taking SOME kind of medication by now!
BATTERY OPERATED TOOTHBRUSH	Use when "Arthur Itis" just won't let you hold your arm up that long.
BOTTLE OF BUBBLES	Never lose the child in you. Let it out once in a while.
PERSONAL FAN	To help you keep your "cool" when the "flashes" hit.
PLASTICWARE	No respectable retiree washes silverware!
STATIC GUARD	Keep those polyester pants from sticking to your knee-high stockings.
LIFE PRESERVER	Use this when you are drowning in free time.
RECORDING KEY CHAIN	Never get lost in the parking lot again.

(Debra Macklin, Quincy, MI)

Card Baskets

People often give retirees greeting cards with gift cards or certificates inside. When there are multiple retirees being honored, make a basket for each one. Use square baskets, weave ribbon around each one, and tie a bow in the front. Stick an artificial flower in the basket. Line the baskets with corresponding colors of tissue paper.

Take head shot pictures of each retiree (especially if you can get them standing in front of an "Exit" sign). Cut out and laminate the pictures. Glue each one to a popsicle stick and attach the sticks to the baskets. (This helps guests put the appropriate card in the basket for each retiree.) *(Debra Macklin, Quincy, MI)*

Chapters of Life

Decorate each table with memorabilia from the various chapters of the retiree's life (e.g., college, career, parent, volunteer, etc.). Include such items as photos, hats, tools, etc. Put a brief narrative on each table to describe the life chapter.

Survival Kits for Retirees

Make a Survival Kit for each staff member who is retiring by placing the following items and the corresponding "instructions" in a plastic bag.

Survival Kit for Retirees

PENNY: To remind you how *lucky you are* to be retired

HAPPY-FACE STICKER: To remind you to *start each day with a smile*

SAD-FACE STICKER: To remind you of *the expression of your "ex-coworkers,"* now that you aren't working with them anymore

RUBBER BAND: To remind you to *stay flexible*; change is never easy

CANDLE: To remind you to *share your light* with others

PENCIL: To remind you to *keep in touch* with your friends

GOLF TEE: To remind you to *play* at something

TEA BAG: To remind you to *relax* and make time for yourself

Egg Hunt

Each year when a staff member retires, the Student Council holds an Egg Hunt for the staff in the gym. Each staff member searches for the egg that has his or her name. In the center of the room is a HUGE chocolate egg for the future retiree. This begins the process for the students to start thanking the retiring staff person

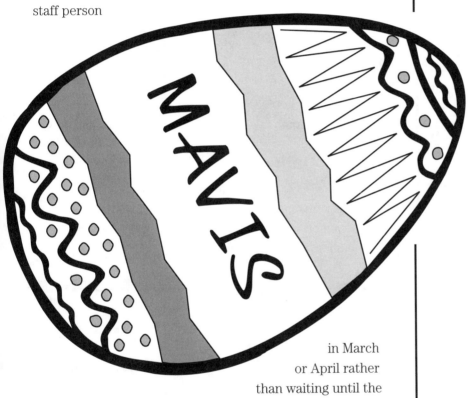

in March or April rather than waiting until the end of the school year. This event usually takes place the day before spring break, so everyone is ready to hunt for eggs. *(Daleville Junior/Senior High School, Daleville, IN)*

In Their Names

Are there several people retiring at your school? Consider giving the following types of gifts in their names:

- Make a donation to the school or a teacher-training university in each person's name

- Give a scholarship donation to students who are going into education
- Donate books to the school or public library in the names of the retirees
- Plant trees on the campus with plaques honoring the retirees

Trivia Quiz

As part of the retirement celebration, create quiz questions about the retiree that attendees can take (e.g., how many years has he or she been employed, in how many districts was he or she employed, how many principals did he or she work with, what hobbies does he or she have, etc.) Invite former coworkers to take part. Winners are given small gifts.

Memory Quilt

Schools often have T-shirts that staff and students wear, and the designs change each year. Save the extra T-shirts and make a memory quilt. This is a wonderful gift for retiring staff members who have worked at the school for many years.

Paw Paw Elementary School 1995–1996	Paw Paw Elementary School 1996–1997	Paw Paw Elementary School 1997–1998
PAW PAW ELEMENTARY SCHOOL 1998–1999	Paw Paw Elementary School 1999–2000	Paw Paw Elementary School 2000–2001
Paw Paw Elementary School 2001–2002	Paw Paw Elementary School 2002–2003	Paw Paw Elementary School 2003–2004

Retirement Schedule

Give the retiree a new schedule for retirement life. Where appropriate, tailor it to fit their particular interests.

RETIREMENT SCHEDULE

7:00 AM	Wake up—listen to the silent alarm clock
7:01 AM	Go back to sleep
7:30 AM	Wake up. Listen to the children going to school and the parents speeding down the street
7:31 AM	Go back to sleep
9:00 AM	Wake up
9:01 to 9:02 AM	Envision yourself jogging or doing sit-ups while lying in bed
9:02 to 10:00 AM	Eat breakfast, read the newspaper
10:00 to 11:00 AM	Make a list of the things to be done that day
11:00 AM to 12:00 PM	Coffee break on the couch
12:00 to 1:00 PM	Lunch (without playground duty!)
1:00 to 1:30 PM	Read a self-help book
1:30 to 3:00 PM	Nap on the couch
3:00 to 4:00 PM	Sit in the rocking chair on the porch and watch the kids come home from school
4:00 to 4:30 PM	Review morning plan and reschedule for tomorrow
4:30 to 6:00 PM	Wave at the neighbors coming home from work
6:00 to 7:00 PM	Cocktail hour, dinner, watch the evening news
7:00 to 8:00 PM	Discuss with your partner all of the things that are wrong in the world
8:00 to 9:00 PM	Put on pajamas and watch TIVO recording of *Wheel of Fortune* and *Jeopardy*
9:00 to 9:10 PM	Write to your former boss and tell your colleagues how much you miss going to work
9:10 to 9:30 PM	Read second self-help book
9:31 PM	Fall asleep
	Recycle

ADMINISTRATIVE PROFESSIONALS DAY

What Professional Assistants Really Want

The International Association of Administrative Professionals (IAAP) conducted a Web poll to find out how people in the administrative professions prefer to observe Administrative Professionals Week, and how it is observed in their offices. Here are the results:

Administrative Professionals Week
Web Poll Results

	% Preferred Observance	% Actual Observance
Companywide observance or special events for administrative staff	26.7	10.4
Training session or education event	22.8	3.6
Bonus or monetary award	13.8	0.8
Day off	11.2	0.2
Optional recognition by individual departments or managers	7.3	36.9
Card or letter of thanks from supervisor or manager	4.7	4.8
Other	4.7	0.0
Lunch	3.9	18.9
Not Observed	3.0	11.8
Candy, flowers, or other gift	1.9	12.7

(International Association of Administrative Professionals, 2005 www.iaap-hq.org)

Students' View of the Job

During Administrative Assistants Week, teachers ask their students to write down what they think the secretary, attendance clerk, workroom assistant, etc., all do in their jobs. The answers are then posted in the lounge for the staff to read and enjoy. *(DeSoto Independent School District, DeSoto, TX)*

What Every Woman Wants

Purchase a huge basket. Prior to Administrative Assistants Day, send a memo to the staff asking each person to bring in an item for the basket that reflects the theme of *"What Every Woman Wants."* Fill the basket with gift certificates for meals, manicures, pedicures, movies, jewelry, decorative items, the DVD of *What Every Woman Wants,* bubble bath, etc. (perhaps even auto services and self-defense classes). Present the basket to the school's administrative assistant and watch the excitement as she discovers all the gifts in the basket.

R-e-l-a-x

We all know that administrative professionals have a direct path to heaven; they are irreplaceable—and are greatly appreciated. On their special day, give them an afternoon of pampering. Make arrangements for these staff members to have manicure or pedicure appointments. Other staff members can cover for administrative assistants while the latter are enjoying their time away from the office. If there is more than one administrative assistant, it is nice that they go together to enjoy each other's company while they RELAX! *(Ross Elementary School, Milford, DE)*

SPRING!!

Spring is Busting Out All Over

A sign that spring is coming is when flowers such as tulips and daffodils start to grow in yards. In anticipation of spring, spread out spring flower bulbs, potting soil, flowerpots, gardening gloves, trowels, water, etc. Encourage staff members to each plant a pot for their classrooms so students can watch for these signs of spring. At the end of the year, plant the bulbs on the school grounds. You could give a prize to the person whose plant bloomed first.

Spring Cleaning

Have a Spring Cleaning Day with your colleagues. This event can be implemented in two ways.

Version #1

Each staff member can bring in two items from home that they want to get rid of. The guidelines are that the person must be able to carry the items into the building and must remove them at the end of the day if no one wants them. On a day when students are not at school, set up tables and display the items. Each staff member is allowed to take two things. If there are items remaining at the end of the day, they are "up for grabs."

Version #2

This version involves classroom supplies. Often there are staff members who are retiring, leaving the school, changing grade levels, etc. Holding a Spring Room Cleaning Day can really help out in these situations. Each person brings items they are no longer using from their classrooms, and displays these classroom "goodies" on tables set up for this event. Staff members can then select items that will be useful for their classrooms. All leftover items can be either donated or disposed of. *(Debra Macklin, Quincy, MI)*

Bloom Where You Are Planted

Make a large flower for each grade level or content area in your school. The center of the flower has the grade level or content area written on it. Each staff member has a petal on which he or she attaches a picture and little-known facts about him- or herself. Display the flowers in the hall during spring.

Frisbee Toss

You will need to plan for this activity in advance. In the middle of winter there will be a "teaser" day: the temperature rises, and it feels like spring is on its way. Put a note on a Frisbee telling everyone to meet at a designated place outside after the students leave. Ask that the Frisbee be "tossed" to other staff members so that everyone gets the message. When the students have left for the day, have multiple Frisbees ready for everyone to toss and then take them home. You may even want to have contests. Play and be merry (for tomorrow it may snow)!

Spring Fever Lunch

After that teaser day when you realize that you actually have months of winter ahead, hold a Spring Fever Lunch. Cover the tables with brightly colored checkered tablecloths and accent them with flowers in watering cans. Decorate with butterflies and ladybugs. Serve hot dogs and hamburgers, and dragonfly-, butterfly-, and bee-shaped sugar cookies.

Provide fun toys such as jump ropes, squirt guns, and jacks. Have an indoor corn toss: Divide the staff into teams of two and give each team an ear of corn. The rules are simple: players have to (1) catch the corn, and (2) take a step back each time they toss the corn to their partner. Give the winning team a gift with a springtime theme.

Parking Lot Lunch

When spring actually does arrive, have a Parking Lot Lunch with a tent and barbeque grills set up. Celebrate the passing of winter and the change of seasons—and attitudes!! A favorite dessert (appropriate for rainy spring weather) is mud pie.

Mud Pie

Chocolate pudding
Oreo cookies, crumbled
Gummy worms and bugs
Terra-cotta flowerpots lined with plastic wrap
Unused plastic beach or garden shovel

Prepare the chocolate pudding according to the package. Fill the lined flowerpot close to the top. Put some of the gummy worms and bugs in and on top of the pudding. Put the shovel in the pudding and sprinkle the crumbled cookies on top.

Plan some outdoor games, such as **Frisbee golf**. Set up the playing area by hanging buckets from trees. Staff members move from bucket to bucket trying to sink the Frisbee (just as golfers move from one hole to the next).

If the weather is conducive, have a **water challenge without guns**. Players can use anything that will hold water (e.g., sponges, spray bottles, turkey basters, cups, balloons, etc.) to soak members of the other teams—but no water guns.

Chapter 9
Holiday Happiness

CHINESE NEW YEAR

The Chinese New Year celebrations begin on the first day of the first month of the Chinese calendar. This is the day of the second new moon after the Winter Solstice. The 15-day celebration includes fireworks, firecrackers, food, candy, and gift-giving.

Festival

Send out invitations to the celebration, decorated with pictures of dragons, firecrackers, other Chinese images, and calligraphy. In your message, include the fact that in the Chinese tradition, red clothes are to be worn to scare away bad fortune.

Transform your meeting area into a Chinese festival venue. Many traditional activities are associated with this holiday; make posters describing the traditions, and display the Chinese calendar. Red and gold are symbols of luck and prosperity, so use them as your color scheme. Place red and black balloons around the room with gold ties.

Because it is tradition to start the New Year with a clean slate, make sure brooms and dustpans are out of sight to prevent good fortune from being swept away.

Set up a buffet with an assortment of Chinese food. At one end of the table, place red plates and chopsticks wrapped with red napkins. At the other end, have beverages (including green tea) available in red cups. When planning the menu, keep in mind traditional dishes with ingredients that have important meanings. Make and display a sign to share these associations:

Dumplings represent **Wealth**

Lettuce represents **Prosperity**

Noodles represent **Longevity**

Oysters represent **Receptivity to Good Fortune**

Seaweed represents **Good Luck**

Whole fish represent **Abundance and Togetherness**

Tangerines are symbolic of good luck and oranges are symbolic of wealth. Serve a tray of fruit for the staff to enjoy.

"Trays of Togetherness" are also part of the celebration. Families keep a tray of dried fruits and candies to share with visiting friends and relatives. Make a tray of goodies to share as well.

And remember the fortune cookies! If you have enough time before the celebration, you can special-order fortune cookies with customized messages.

Flowers also play an important role in the celebration. Peonies symbolize love, affection, and beauty. Use silk flowers to adorn the buffet table or put in vases on the dining tables. (One of the traditional beliefs: if a peach blossom blooms during the New Year celebration, good fortune is ahead.) String flower garlands around the room.

Another tradition during this time: "Lai-See envelopes" are red envelopes given by senior members of a family to junior members. Each small envelope contains a small amount of money. Employers could also give red envelopes to their employees on the first working day after the festival. Give staff members token envelopes that have "school currency" in them, e.g., free lunch in the cafeteria, leave-early certificate, etc.

Display the Chinese zodiac symbols: Year of the Dog, Year of the Tiger, etc. Staff members will naturally want to find out which animal they are, based on their birth year. This can make for fun discussions.

Parades are also part of the tradition with dragons, firecrackers, and fireworks. Note: This level of celebration requires a lot of preparation and can sometimes be hard to include in staff activities.

GROUNDHOG DAY

Groundhog Day Celebration

Each year Punxsutawney Phil peeks out of his hole and looks for his shadow. If he sees it, there are six more weeks of winter ahead. No matter what the outcome, have a fun celebration of this event.

Go to www.punxsutawneyphil.com to find and e-mail free Groundhog Day postcards to staff members, inviting them to your gathering.

At your celebration, serve "groundhog food": seeds, lettuce, and salad. You may want to have some other types of food in another part of the room to keep everybody happy.

Check www.groundhog.org for activity suggestions. They have fun Groundhog Bingo games and sing-along songs, including "I'm Dreaming of a Great Groundhog" (to the tune of "White Christmas") and "Groundhog Wonderland" (to the tune of "Winter Wonderland"). Of course you could always show the movie *Groundhog Day*, starring Bill Murray.

VALENTINE'S DAY

Valentine String Hunt

Divide the staff into teams of two or three. Cut red and pink yarn or string into various lengths and hide the strands all over the school. Staff members search for the string throughout the day. Periodically, they meet up with their team members and tie the pieces of string together to make one long, continuous piece of string. Staff members gather at the end of the day and find out which team made the longest string. The winning team is given a Valentine's Day prize.

Special Delivery

Provide all the fixings to decorate heart-shaped cookies. Have staff members write special messages to their coworkers on the cookies (if a message is too long, it can be written on a card). Put the cookies in plastic bags and have them delivered to the designated staff member on Valentine's Day.

Words of Praise and Affection

Make bookmarks with nice messages on them.

Using a laser printer, print short messages on a sheet of translucent vellum (e.g., *XOXOXO, You Make Everyone Smile, You Have a Great Big Heart for Everyone!*). Cut out red cardstock to the size you want for the bookmark. Trim the vellum to the same size, making sure the message is centered on the bookmark. Layer the vellum over the paper and punch a hole in the top. Bind both sheets together with satin ribbon.

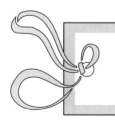

WORLD'S BEST VALENTINE!

Flowery Praise

Give each staff member a rose and personalized message telling why you "love" working with them.

Secret Valentine

Write the name of a staff member on a Valentine's card and display the cards where staff members congregate (e.g., lunchroom, mailboxes, etc.). Staff members select a Valentine and then "lavish" that person with gifts. Throughout the week of Valentine's Day, give the person fun, inexpensive gifts—and enjoy being a Secret Valentine! *(Colorado State University, Ft. Collins, CO)*

MARDI GRAS MADNESS

Bourbon Street Parade

Schedule a Mardi Gras gathering, complete with floats. A week before the celebration, divide the staff members into working groups and give each group a cart to transform into a float. It can carry staff members who dress up for the occasion, wear creative masks, and give out beads. (You can also provide beads, feathers, string, paper, etc., for staff members to make their own masks.) Decorate the hall in a Bourbon Street theme and play live or recorded Dixieland jazz music. Have the floats parade down the hall for judging. The winning team gets a New Orleans-style prize. Celebrate after the parade with Cajun or Southern food (e.g., gumbo, hush puppies).

ST. PATRICK'S DAY

Lucky Pots of Gold Search

Make "pots of gold" and put a staff member's name on each one. Hide the pots all over the school. When the staff member finds the pot with his or her name, that person gets a prize. *(Debra Macklin, Quincy, MI)*

A little green man got in here last night.
He brought pots of gold to stir your delight.
Everyone gets one; no one's been left out,
But you must find yours—they're hidden all about.
Locate the pot that bears your name
And you'll be a winner in this game.
Take it to an administrator of your choice
To receive a prize that will make you rejoice!
Happy St. Patrick's Day!

Pot of Gold Search

Make a large pot of gold out of poster board. In the center, draw a circle divided into eight sections and add an arrow spinner (this will look similar to the wheel in *Wheel of Fortune*). Place a picture of a prize or "Choice" on each of the sections. Display the board in the office.

Create a master list of clues that feature clever word play. Give the instructions with the clues. Below are examples of clues (some of these are specific to Jennings Elementary School, Quincy, MI, but they will serve as "idea starters"). The answers are in parentheses for your use only—don't give them to staff members.

Instructions: Figure out where these clues are hidden to get another clue. Find a St. Patrick's Day sticker, take it to the office to get a chance to spin for a prize on the Pot of Gold Wheel, and see if you have the luck of the Irish!

1. Multicolored bodies hide a clue.
   One teacher has life-sized paper cut-outs of her students outside her room.

2. The tallest room in the school holds a clue.
   The library, because it has a lot of "stories."

3. If you go ape you might miss a clue.
   There is a large stuffed ape by the front door.

4. If you find a clue you're on a roll.
   Large rolls of paper on a stand

5. You might seal the deal with a clue.
   A laminator

6. If you look in the write place you'll find a clue.
   Book/pencil/eraser machine

7. Remember, when you're looking for a clue, don't leaf any stone unturned.
   There are two large plants by the front door.

8. You could call for help, but it will cost you.
   Pay phone

9. You can find a clue, even if the trail is cold.
   Soda machine—"can" and "cold" are the clues.

10. If a cook asks to help, letter help you find a clue.
    There is a mailbox that food service uses to collect lunch money.

11. You'll find a clue when you quench your desire for fun.
    Water fountain

12. Don't reproduce your clues.
    Photocopier

13. Go here if you need a rest from clues.
    Staff restroom

14. Finding a clue is as easy as opening your mind to outside influences.
    Outside doors

15. Don't give up looking if you find yourself lost.
    Lost and found

16. Get the point and feel the power.
    A "PowerPoint" sign is displayed outside the technology room.

17. Don't get sick of looking.
    The health room

18. Sometimes finding clues is like catching fish without worms.
    There is a basket of "play fish" that are thrown around when staff are stressed.

19. Don't let the lady bug you while looking for clues.
    There is a large ladybug at the front counter.

20. Flag someone down if you need help looking for clues.
    There is a large flag outside of the office.

Clue #1: Give the clue list to all staff members, and tell them they can start with any of the clues. When they have deciphered the message, they go to that location and find a small envelope with a green clover sticker on the front. Inside is another clue that gives them instructions on where to find the final clue—Clue #2 (e.g., "Look under the chair by the front door" or "Look on page 2 of *The Cat in the Hat* book in the library.")

Clue #2: Clue #2 consists of a St. Patrick's Day sticker and instructions to bring it to the office, where they get a chance to spin the Pot of Gold Wheel and win prizes.
(Debra Macklin, Quincy, MI)

Wee Bit O' Fun

Of course on St. Patrick's Day everyone will want to wear green. Have a social gathering in which you send out the notice attached to a minibox of Lucky Charms cereal.

Serve fun green food items (and remember that you can make just about anything green by simply adding food coloring).

- Salad
- Clover-shaped sandwiches (use clover cookie cutters)
- Green clover-shaped cake
- Mint or green tea ice cream
- A "Pot of Gold" filled with chocolate coins wrapped in gold foil
- Lime Jell-O
- Green grapes

Four-Leaf Clover Praise

Cut out a four-leaf clover for each staff member. Write on it four positive comments about that person (e.g., Your smile lights up the school, You are a GREAT secretary, Your enthusiasm is contagious, You are a gift for these kids!).

EASTER

Marshmallow Easter Eggs

Make Easter treats for the staff meeting using this recipe.

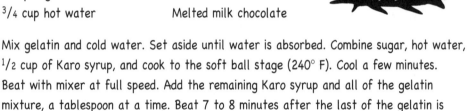

Marshmallow Easter Eggs

2 tbsp Knox gelatin	1 cup white Karo syrup
$^1/_2$ cup cold water	2 tsp vanilla
2 cup sugar	Corn starch for hands
$^3/_4$ cup hot water	Melted milk chocolate

Mix gelatin and cold water. Set aside until water is absorbed. Combine sugar, hot water, $^1/_2$ cup of Karo syrup, and cook to the soft ball stage (240° F). Cool a few minutes. Beat with mixer at full speed. Add the remaining Karo syrup and all of the gelatin mixture, a tablespoon at a time. Beat 7 to 8 minutes after the last of the gelatin is added. Add vanilla.

Pour into a well-greased 7" x 9" pan and chill thoroughly. Dust hands with cornstarch. Spoon the marshmallow out of the pan and form eggs. Brush excess corn starch off and let dry for $^1/_2$ hour on waxed paper. Pour melted milk chocolate over eggs and let stand. Refrigerate for easier handling.

Peeps Jousting

In the spring, marshmallow chickens called "Peeps" are found in grocery stores. As a faculty room activity, give each person a Peep and a toothpick. You will also need a microwave oven.

"Knights" (staff members) name their chicks, stick "lances" (toothpicks) in them, and pop them into the microwave. Turn on the power; the last chick standing is named the "Master Knight."

Eggciting Search

When staff members are out of the building, visit their class-rooms or workstations. Hide a plastic egg filled with candy and an Easter greeting for them to find. Stamp some of the messages with a star or smile. The people who get these eggs receive a special gift appropriate for the holiday.

Put the following poem in a visible spot so everyone can read about the event.

(Debra Macklin, Quincy, MI)

There is no Easter
Bunny, some silly people say.
No Bunny can lay all those eggs
in a day.
No Bunny can hide all that
candy about.
But we say "phooey" to those
who would doubt.

We know he exists, and though we've
not heard him shout
We have found some "Eggciting" clues hidden about.
If you look around, you are sure to find
An egg of the most interesting kind.

It could be hidden anywhere in your space.
It might even be in an obvious place.
Inside it a special message will be found
And something sweet that weighs less than a pound.

If your message is stamped with a smile or a star
Dash down to the office, you don't need a car.
When you get there you will be
allowed to choose
A fabulous gift—you see—
you can't lose!

Happy Easter!!

APRIL FOOL'S DAY

April Fool's Treats

Host a gathering in which the food is "interesting." Two menu items could be a Kitty Litter Cake and Puppy Chow.

Kitty Litter Cake

1 box spice or German chocolate cake mix
1 box of white cake mix
1 package white sandwich cookies
1 large package vanilla instant pudding mix
Green food coloring
12 small Tootsie Rolls

1 NEW cat litter box
1 NEW cat litter box liner
1 NEW pooper scooper

Prepare and bake cake mixes according to directions, in any size pan. Prepare pudding and chill. Crumble cookies in small batches in blender or food processor. Add a few drops of green food coloring to 1 cup of cookie crumbs. Mix with a fork or shake in a jar. Set aside.

When cakes are at room temperature, crumble them into a large bowl. Toss with half of the remaining cookie crumbs and enough pudding to make the mixture moist but not soggy. Place liner in litter box and pour in mixture.

Unwrap 3 Tootsie Rolls and heat in a microwave until soft and pliable. Shape blunt ends into slightly curved points. Repeat with 3 more rolls. Bury the rolls decoratively in the cake mixture. Sprinkle remaining white cookie crumbs over the mixture, then scatter green crumbs over top.

Heat 5 more Tootsie Rolls until almost melted. Put them on top of the cake and sprinkle with crumbs from the litter box. Heat the remaining Tootsie Roll until pliable, and hang it over the edge of the box.

Place box on a sheet of newspaper and serve with scooper.

PUPPY CHOW

2 cups chocolate chips

1 (15 ounce) box Crispix or Rice Chex

1 cup peanut butter

1/2 cup margarine

3 cups confectioners' sugar

Place chocolate chips, peanut butter, and margarine in a glass bowl. Heat in a microwave on High until melted. Mix well. Combine cereal and chocolate mix. Stir until coated. Place confectioners' sugar in a bag, add cereal mix, and shake to coat. Spread on wax paper. Let stand until set. Serves 10.

Warning: This "puppy chow" is not good for dogs. Don't feed it to them.

 # CINCO DE MAYO

Cinco de Mayo is the celebration of the Battle of Puebla on May 5, 1862, in which the Mexican Army defeated the French Army. Although the holiday is often confused in the U.S. with Mexican Independence, Mexican independence from Spain was actually declared much earlier on September 16, 1810.

Fiesta

Celebrate Mexican culture by having a Cinco de Mayo fiesta. Send staff colorful invitations decorated with pictures of the Mexican flag, chilies, etc. Or you can prepare all of the information in an artistic flier and roll it into a tube shape.

Transform the lounge into a colorful fiesta site. Decorate with chili pepper wreaths, etc. The colors of the Mexican flag are red, white, and green, so incorporate those colors into your decorations through balloons, raffia to tie napkins, paper plates and cups, etc. Mexican blankets make great tablecloths or wall hangings.

Play Mexican music during the meal. Serve Mexican foods, such as chili con queso, chicken lime soup, fajitas, tacos, guacamole, salsa, pinto beans, Mexican rice, and flan.

Salsa/Hot Sauce Contest

Hold a Salsa/Hot Sauce Contest as part of the fiesta. Each person prepares his or her favorite recipe for other staff members to taste. Have a large supply of tortilla chips available (but no double dipping!). Ask for volunteers to serve as judges to select winners in various categories, e.g., mild, medium, hot, and fire! Have each participant make multiple copies of his or her recipe to share with colleagues.

FOURTH OF JULY CELEBRATION

Have a staff celebration of the Fourth of July. This could occur during the traditional school year with the teachers (on a fictitious day) or with the staff members who work during the summer. It could include a picnic with hot dogs, corn on the cob, popsicles, and watermelon slices.

The event could also include competitions such as a watermelon seed spitting contest and a hot dog eating contest (using cocktail hot dogs). And don't forget the three-legged races!

But the main event should be the Fourth of July parade. Prior to the event, staff members are divided into working groups to build floats for the parade. The captains meet to learn about the rules of the event and to draw their vehicle. The names of vehicles are put on pieces of paper and put in a hat for each captain to select. Examples of vehicles include a lawnmower, tricycle, bicycle, wheelchair, motorcycle, scooter, wagon, etc. Each group is given a predetermined budget and time line in which to decorate its float. The floats are paraded and judged, and prizes are awarded. Musical staff members can also march in the parade, or wagons with CD players can provide the music. Participants and viewers alike can dress up like Uncle Sam. Include toy fire trucks or military vehicles to enhance the celebration.

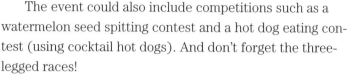 LABOR DAY

Haywire Holiday

Sometimes the best of plans go haywire. After a long weekend or holiday break, ask members to share their traumas by completing the following sentence.

My Labor Day Weekend (or other holiday) was going great until _____.

Examples of holidays gone haywire include:

. . . I got a call from my mother asking me to drive her to the hospital. She was coming out of church, looking in her purse for sunglasses, missed the step, and broke her foot.

. . . my son dislocated his shoulder playing football with his cousins.

. . . I tried to light the grill and found that it was out of gas—and we had 20 people at our house for a barbeque.

. . . the outdoor picnic was infested with a huge swarm of bees. Everyone had to move inside, and we don't have a house large enough to accommodate that number of people.

Staff members can turn in their entries for judging. At the staff meeting, read the most interesting ones and let people guess who submitted them. You might want to award a funny prize to the person who was judged as having the worst experience.

HALLOWEEN SPOOKTACULAR EVENTS

Pumpkin Bowling

Modify a child's bowling game by decorating the pins to look like pumpkin faces. Arrange the pumpkins in the triangular order of bowling pins as shown below.

Each person gets a chance to knock down the pumpkins. Throughout the day, staff members throw two balls, count the number of pumpkins they toppled, and then record the number on a score sheet. At the end of the day, the staff members who tie for the highest score have a "bowl-off." You may want to increase the difficulty by moving the line farther away from the pins. The winner gets an appropriate Halloween gift.

Pumpkin Smashing

Smashing pumpkins is done frequently by children on Halloween night—and makes a mess. Have your own pumpkin-smashing activity, but one that is fun and not destructive. Clean out a pumpkin and let it dry for several days. Fill it with all kinds of fun candy and treats. Take the staff outside and have a volunteer drop the pumpkin from the roof of the school. Staff members then get to gather up the treats and candy, and can enjoy them with the Witch's Brew (below).

Witch's Brew

Fill a plastic glove with water or punch. Adding a contrasting food color may be helpful. Tie off the opening of the glove with a rubber band or wire. Put the glove in the freezer until the liquid is frozen solid. Carefully remove the glove, place the frozen hand in the punch bowl ("cauldron"), and add soda or punch.

Ghostly Gifts

When staff members have gone home, visit their classrooms or workstations. Hide a ghostly figure made out of construction paper or cheese cloth for them to find. Put the following poem in a visible location so they know to look for the ghost. When they have found the goblin, they bring it to the office for a Halloween treat. *(Debra Macklin, Quincy, MI)*

While walking past the school last night
My eyes beheld a frightful sight.
On the wind floated a mournful sound
And a shimmering mist swirled all around.
I think there may have been spooks in there
But enter and check? I did not dare!
So if you find your space is haunted
Capture the specter; you must be undaunted.
Bring it to the office—don't delay
And a sweet reward will come your way!

Ghostly Praise

Make ghost suckers out of Tootsie Roll Pops and facial tissue. Attach a note such as "We don't stand a 'ghost' of a chance of achievement without you!"

Biting for Apples

As an alternative to bobbing for apples, have a "biting for apples" contest. Attach thread to the stems of the apples and hang them from the ceiling. Hang one apple for each participant and let them try to take a bite out of their apple.

Fall Harvest

Assemble a package of pumpkin candies and attach a note of appreciation such as "Thank you for 'harvesting' our students' potential."

Mummy Wrap

Divide the staff into teams or pairs. Give each group a roll of toilet paper and have them try to mummify (wrap up) each other in a race to be first. Warning: The faster you go, the quicker the paper tears. The winning team gets a Halloween treat.

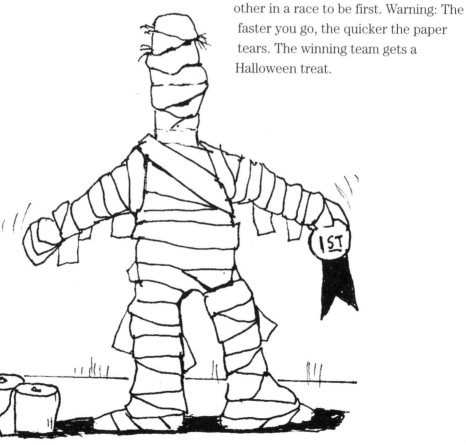

Halloween Scavenger Hunt

For this scavenger hunt, divide the staff into teams and assign each team a color.

Look for the place where there sits a pot,
but filled with witch's brew it's not.
Choose one team member to be the one
who can't stop trying until the job is done.

Fill a "cauldron" or pot with Jell-O that has been stirred after it has set. Stir in small Styrofoam or plastic balls with eyes drawn on them. Color each "eye" with the color of each team. Give the chosen team member a latex glove. Without looking, he or she is to feel around in the pot until he or she finds the eye with the color of the team.

Next you must find among the leaves and hidden behind
a dismembered foot.
It's high in the tree, not down near the root.

Make a large tree out of paper. Hang lots of leaves that are attached at the top so they can be flipped up. Place each team's color under a leaf. Team members have to flip up leaves until they find the one with their color underneath.

Now you must find a loose set of lips.
Get started looking, and I'll give you some tips.
Look for the talking head that won't quit.
Grab your lips, but be careful or you may get bit.

Have someone sit on a stool or chair and make that person's head look bloody. Place a box with a hole cut in it over his or her head to serve as the "table." Cover it with a tablecloth to hide the rest of the person's body. Have this "talking head" chatter constantly and attempt to bite at those looking for the lips. From behind the talking head have someone in a long

overcoat recite the following (use chainsaw sound effects to add to the mood):

Once upon a time, a long time ago
I chopped off the head of a fellow that I know.
As I plucked out his teeth he started to yell.
So I ripped off his lips and silent he fell.
But what did I ever do with those lips?
Did I put them in the pocket of my shirt
or inside my shoe and closer to the dirt?
Find the lips in your color if you're able
or you'll end up like him, over there on the table.

Put the lips (one in the color of each team) inside the overcoat of the person reciting the verse. He or she could perform flasher-type moves to give the teams a hint as to where the lips can be found.

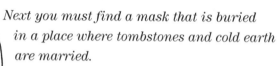

Next you must find a mask that is buried
in a place where tombstones and cold earth
are married.
Look for the place where you should be most wary
Start digging within the old cemetery.

Set up fake tombstones and pile leaves all around them. Under the leaves, hide masks with each team's color. Team members dig through the leaves to find their mask.

As the night moon slips low
pumpkin faces will glow.
Deep within, where the pumpkin bleeds
you must reach and find a bag full of seeds.
Make sure you get your team's shade
or a reach into another must be made.

Put pumpkin seeds in zippered plastic bags and hide in uncarved pumpkins with the tops cut out. Make sure to put each team's color on each bag. Use several pumpkins so players have to try more than once to find their seeds.

Somewhere near stagnant water and mud
are severed hands tinged with blood.
They float unattached to the bodies they knew
like hideous dumplings in bloody stew.

Ahead of time, fill latex gloves with water. Add
food coloring so that one glove matches each
team's color. The others can be filled with plain
water. A red permanent marker can be used to
simulate blood around the wrist area. Use a
kiddie pool with cold water and a little red food
coloring with leaves floating on top. Team members have to grab the hand in their color.

Further down the walk you will creep if you're wise.
Find the silk spun in the doorway by a creature of
great size.
Look for a spider in your color.
Don't grab the spider of another.

Use spider webbing in a dark doorway. Hang lots of
spiders on the web with the colors of the teams
underneath (one for each team); this can be done with
colored tape or markers. Team members must find their
spider. For effect, you could have two small lights
resembling eyes glowing from behind the web.

Next the location of a prize pumpkin must be found.
Search for Halloween bags on the ground.
Look in the bags and dig through the leaves
Find your color and run like thieves.

Use several small plastic pumpkins (or small pumpkin gourds)
and mark with one color for each team. Place in one of
several Halloween pumpkin trash bags. Team members then
have to dig through the bags to find their pumpkin.

Look to the sky for bodies of no shape.
Creepy little ghosts to leave your mouth agape.

Grab the one that's colored in your
team's shade.
Try hard to be brave, to not be afraid.

Hang ghosts from the ceiling. Place each team's
color on a ghost. Team members have to find and
retrieve their ghost.

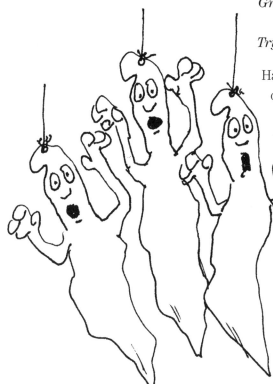

Left to blow upon the wind
hang the bones of Thomas Lynd.
He was left here one full moon night
to die alone before morning's light.
It's long since past when he had a need.
There is no skin from which to bleed.
So retrieve the bone in the color you're used to,
but leave his head intact or he'll forever haunt you.

Hang a paper skeleton from the ceiling or a
doorway. Mark one bone with the color for each
team. Team members must retrieve their
bone.

You've made it past the witch's pot
and weren't held back by the stench of rot.
The blood head didn't scare you away.
You found the lips, pumpkin, and mask
in one day.
The others you found along the way.
The gore is over, this game is now done.
This is the time when you find what you've won.

Make a cardboard "coffin." Fill it with prizes
or Halloween or classroom supplies, and allow each
team that has collected all of the souvenirs
to choose a prize. *(Debra Macklin, Quincy, MI)*

THANKSGIVING

"Talkin' Turkey" Bingo

On the morning before Thanksgiving break, give each staff member a bingo card containing 3–6 games. The numbers are called during student passing periods so that time is not taken away from instruction. When a staff member gets a "BINGO," the winner calls the office, and a student runner brings the card to be verified. The student selects a prize donated from local vendors for the winning staff member to take it back to the classroom.

Words of Thanks

Make paper cut-outs in the shape of turkey feathers. Write a personal note to each staff member telling why you are thankful that he or she is on the staff.

Surprise Pies

Have an assortment of pies (including pumpkin, of course!) in the staff lounge for staff members to enjoy. You could also give each person their favorite pie to take home for the holiday to enjoy with their families.

WINTER HOLIDAYS DECORATING

Winter Wonderland

Prior to winter break, the administrators come in on a weekend and transform the staff lounge into a "Winter Wonderland." The room is enlivened with colorful, festive holiday decorations, lights, candles, tablecloths, and music. Stockings are personalized for every staff member, filled with treats, and hung from a clothesline. Throughout the week the staff is treated to breakfast and lunch buffets, encouraged to take part in sing-alongs, etc. Each staff member also receives a gift.

Winter Holiday Celebration

Decorate the auditorium or cafeteria with decorations of the season and host a holiday breakfast. Invite the neighboring high school choir to perform holiday songs and/or ask parents to perform. It is a lovely community gathering to put everyone in the holiday spirit. *(Bear Lake Elementary School, Apopka, FL)*

Make an Ornament

Host a gathering and supply raw materials (e.g., glass or Styrofoam balls, string, sequins, pins, wire, glitter, glue, ribbons, paint, scissors, construction paper, etc.). Have each person make a holiday ornament(s) and hang it on the tree.

Decorate the Tree

Display a tree where staff members congregate. Give the tree a different character each year by having the staff select a theme for the decorations (e.g., teddy bears, your school colors, homemade ornaments, college logos, etc.). Each staff member brings in an ornament(s) for the tree. What do you do with the ornaments after the holiday? They can be saved for decorating additional trees, or given to community organizations. You can also hold a drawing for staff members to select an ornament to keep, or the ornaments can be used as door prizes for future staff meetings.

Ornament Search

Make paper ornaments and hide them around the school for a week. The three individuals who collect the most ornaments are given an afternoon off on a designated day to go holiday shopping.

HOLIDAY GIFTS AND EXCHANGES

Pajama-Grams

Make cutouts of pajamas and label each one with the gender and age of a child. Create a display of the pajamas and allow staff members to select one. Each person then buys a pair of pajamas and an age-specific book for a bedtime story. On a designated date, collect these boxed gifts and either deliver them to needy families or take them to an agency or community group for delivery.

Wrapped Up

The school adopts needy families and staff members bring in unwrapped gifts. Basic gift-wrapping paper, tape, and ribbons are provided, but "extras" can also be added to make presents even more festive. Grade-level teams divide the gifts and wrap them. Impartial judges vote on which group receives the "Best Wrapped-Up Award" and the winners receive a special prize. *(Eastside Elementary School, Warren, AR)*

Shoebox Gifts

Throughout the year, collect empty shoeboxes and attach a note to each box with the age and gender of a child (e.g., 3-year old, girl). Give interested staff members one of these boxes and ask them to fill it with items that children need and want such as toys, treats, socks, toothbrushes, etc. The shoeboxes can also be decorated. On a designated date, collect the boxes and either deliver them to needy families or take them to an agency or community group for delivery.

Gifts That Keep on Giving

For the holidays, have staff members draw names for a gift exchange. Each person then researches interests of the person whose name was selected and purchases a toy, game, or gift consistent with his or her preferences. Hold the gift exchange during a group activity; this is sure to result in some fun and laughs. Afterward, collect the gifts and donate them to a charitable organization or families in the district.

Gifts of Time

Before the holiday break, volunteers work in the classrooms for two hours to give teachers time to shop, have lunch, etc.

Catalog Shopping

Host a holiday catalog shopping event for staff members. Contact between four and eight local, in-home catalog party demonstrators (e.g., Pampered Chef, Home & Garden, Mary Kay, tupperware, etc.), depending on the size of the group.

Version #1: Have catalogs available for everyone to use while shopping.

Version #2: Along with the catalogs, have each demonstrator display new items on tables set up around the room.

Have each person make a "Wish List" of three or more items they want, but didn't purchase. Share this list with the person's friends and family as a way to help provide ideas (or hints).

Ask vendors to donate door prizes or have cute, inexpensive items to give away. *(Tanya Blehm, Saginaw, MI)*

Regifting

After the holiday vacation, have staff members rewrap a gift they received. Decide in advance if the gifts are to be useful or gag gifts. The gift exchange may be implemented in different ways.

Version #1: Number each gift. Each staff member then draws a number and selects the corresponding gift.

Version #2: Staff members draw numbers. The person with "1" gets to select a present from the stack. The person who drew "2" is next, and so on.

 JUST FOR FUN

It Just Keeps Going and Going

Purchase three identical battery-operated toys (e.g., drummers playing drums) and three different brands of batteries such as Duracell, Energizer, and Kirkland. Put a different set of batteries in each toy and label the toy to identify which batteries are inside.

Start a "prediction pool" in which each person guesses which toy will run down last, and when it will happen (day and time).

The toys are all started at the same time and placed in a location where they can be monitored. They are turned off at the end of the work day and restarted again in the morning.

The winner is the person whose guess is closest to the actual date and time without going over.

If there is no winner, the person who guessed closest to the date and time (even if the guess was over) wins. Half the money goes to the winner, and the other half goes to a children's organization, or to help support a needy family.

Here Comes Santa Claus

An alarm goes off, and the students scramble outside to welcome Santa. Each year is a surprise as he arrives in a different mode of transportation (e.g., fire truck, ambulance, limousine, helicopter, dump truck, sheriff's car, etc.). Each staff member has his or her picture taken with Santa. The principal encloses the picture in a card that is sent to the staff member's parents, spouse, significant other, etc., with a note of appreciation for that person's contribution to the school.

Holiday Hat Activity Game

Everyone wears a hat symbolic of the season. This game centers on observation. Announce that the rule is that no one may take off his or her hat until you have taken off yours. If you play this game during a staff meeting or gathering, encourage others to begin the normal conversation. People will slowly forget they are in the game. Eventually remove your hat and watch as others figure this out. There will be quick movements, laughs, and giggles as hats come off. One nonobservant person involved in a conversation or activity will be the last to notice. An appropriate prize is given to the "loser." This game can be repeated if time allows.

Holiday Trivia

Divide the staff members into teams. Give them the following quiz and tell them to pick the correct answers. (Be sure to remove the answers from the quiz first.) You can do this as an afterschool event, in which case the winner would be the first team with a correct answer. You could also give the worksheet to each group in the morning or at the beginning of the week and have them work on it over a period of time. If there are multiple groups with correct answers, hold a drawing to determine which team receives the prize.

Movie Trivia

1. In the movie *Scrooged* (1988), Bill Murray plays a character who is a cold-hearted —
   a. principal
   b. television executive
   c. police officer
   d. politician

2. What is the name of George Bailey's guardian angel in the 1946 movie, *It's a Wonderful Life?*
   a. Sabrina
   b. Gerry
   c. Clarence
   d. Sam

3. The film, *It's a Wonderful Life,* shows George Bailey as a child. As a boy he suffered an injury to his —
   a. chest
   b. back
   c. eyes
   d. ear

4. The 1954 film, *White Christmas,* takes place in —
   a. Colorado
   b. Connecticut
   c. Upstate New York
   d. Vermont

5. Who plays Bing Crosby's Army buddy in *White Christmas?*
   a. Jimmy Stewart
   b. Fred Astaire
   c. Danny Kaye
   d. Bob Hope

6. The child who is skeptical about Santa Claus in *Miracle on 34th Street* is played by —

    a. Natalie Wood   c. Shirley Temple

    b. Audrey Hepburn   d. Drew Barrymore

7. *Miracle on 34th Street* features which department store?

    a. Bloomingdale's   c. Marshall Field's

    b. Macy's   d. Saks Fifth Avenue

8. In the 1990 film, *Home Alone,* an eight-year old boy is accidentally left behind while his family flies to a holiday vacation in —

    a. California   c. Paris

    b. London   d. New York

9. What happens to the character played by Tim Allen in the 1994 film, *The Santa Clause?* He —

    a. gains weight   c. gets fired

    b. grows a beard   d. all of the above

10. In the 1994 movie, *Christmas Vacation,* Clark Griswald (played by Chevy Chase) is anxiously awaiting the arrival of —

    a. reindeer   c. relatives

    b. his holiday bonus check   d. New Year's Eve

Answers:

1. b. television executive

2. c. Clarence

3. d. ear

4. d. Vermont

5. c. Danny Kaye

6. a. Natalie Wood

7. b. Macy's

8. c. Paris

9. d. all of the above

10. b. holiday bonus check

Chapter 10
The 12 Days Before the Holiday/Winter Break

PLANNING

Encourage staff members to take part in events during the weeks before the holiday break. You could call them "The 12 Days Before the Holiday/Winter Break," "The 12 Days of Caring," or a name specific to your school or district, such as "The 12 Days of _____ High School Cheer." Staff members may participate in all or selected events. The activities are intended to build comaraderie, generate laughter, contribute good-will, and heighten a holiday spirit.

Planning Committee

Begin planning the holiday events just after Halloween. Ask for volunteers—representatives from each employee group (e.g., administrators, teachers, support staff, etc.)—to serve on a planning committee. Brainstorm the types of events you want to have, letting members volunteer to lead the event of their choice. Assign at least one person to be in charge of communications.

The following example of activities suggests four days designated for each of the ***Secret Santa*** days, ***Group Activity*** days, and for ***Community Caring*** events. A possible sequence of events could be:

Day 1	**_Secret Santa Day . . ._**
	Treat Day
Day 2	**_Group Activity Day . . ._**
	Holiday Sing-along & Name That Tune
Day 3	**_Community Caring Day . . ._**
	Dress a Child Day
Day 4	**_Secret Santa Day . . ._**
	Holiday Ornament Day
Day 5	**_Group Activity Day . . ._**
	Candy Cane Hunt
Day 6	**_Community Caring Day . . ._**
	Family Gift Day
Day 7	**_Secret Santa Day . . ._**
	Stress Reliever Day
Day 8	**_Group Activity Day . . ._**
	Slippers and Cocoa
Day 9	**_Community Caring Day . . ._**
	Build a Holiday Dinner
Day 10	**_Group Activity Day . . ._**
	Build a Snowman
Day 11	**_Community Caring Day . . ._**
	Decorate a Tree/Wrap Gifts
Day 12	**_Secret Santa Day . . ._**
	Potluck Luncheon/Toy Day

Communication

- At an all-staff meeting, describe the planned activities. Allow committee members to present the activity/event they will be in charge of. Emphasize that participation is voluntary.
- Each week, include reminders of the events in the daily announcements.

Monday	Tuesday	Wednesday	Thursday	Friday
			DAY 1 *Secret Santa* Treat Day	**DAY 2** *Group Activity* Holiday Sing-along
DAY 3 *Community Caring* Dress a Child Day	**DAY 4** *Secret Santa* Ornament Day	**DAY 5** *Group Activity* Candy Cane Hunt	**DAY 6** *Community Caring* Family Gift Day	**DAY 7** *Secret Santa* Stress Reliever Day
DAY 8 *Group Activity* Slippers & Cocoa	**DAY 9** *Community Caring* Build a Holiday Dinner	**DAY 10** *Group Activity* Build a Snowman	**DAY 11** *Community Caring* Decorate Tree/Wrap Gifts	**DAY 12** *Secret Santa* Pot Luck/Toy Day
		Vacation!		

- Take pictures at the events and post them where staff members frequent; write relevant articles and submit them to the district and local newspapers.
- Prepare and distribute a calendar of events and display it wherever staff members congregate (e.g., by the mailboxes, in the lounge, restrooms, etc.).

COMMUNITY CARING DAYS

Contact school counselors or social workers, local assistance agencies, or places of worship to get names of families who need help during the holidays. Obtain the clothing and shoe sizes, ages, and genders of each family member. Ask what the children have on their "Wish Lists." Then plan the following Community Caring activities for these recipients.

- Dress a Child Day
- Family Gift Day
- Build a Holiday Dinner Day
- Decorate a Tree/Wrap Gifts Day
- Deliver the Holiday Items to the Families

Dress a Child Day

Make a holiday tree display with paper ornaments as decorations, and write the name of a clothing item, size, gender, and age of the recipient (e.g., Sweater, Child Size 10, Girl, Age 10) on each ornament. Have staff members select a clothing item(s) they would like to contribute. More expensive items such as jeans and shoes could be jointly purchased by multiple staff members.

On the designated day, staff members place the paper ornament on the unwrapped clothing item and put them in a (secured) location, such as under a holiday tree in the staff lounge. At the end of the day, move the items to a location where they can be gift wrapped later on.

Sweater, Girl, Size 10, Age 10

Family Gift Day

Make a list of the demographics of each family the school is sponsoring, listing ages and gender of all family members (remember that pets are family members, too!). If you have pictures of the family, include them as well.

Post the list in the lounge so that staff members can sign up to bring in a gift for a designated person (ensure that all family members receive gifts).

Build a Holiday Dinner Day

Make a list of food items that go into making a holiday dinner. Post a sign-up sheet for the various ingredients or have staff members randomly draw the names of the item(s) out of a hat.

Possible items that can be included are:

• Canned nuts	• Canned fruit
• Canned ham	• Flour
• Turkey	• Sugar
• Canned vegetables	• Salad dressing
• Potatoes	• Stuffing mix
• Bread	• Dessert item(s)

Additional nonperishable items such as cold cereal, oatmeal, granola bars, soup, pasta, spaghetti sauce, instant potatoes, popcorn, cookies, etc., can be contributed for the families. Produce and dairy products can also be brought in if they can be delivered to the families quickly.

Decorate a Tree/Wrap Gifts Day

Obtain small, transportable, fresh or artificial trees, empty baskets (for food), and wrapping paper, ribbon, and tags.

Set the mood with holiday music and divide the participants into three groups.

- One group will make items such as bows, stars, etc., to use as decorations on the tree(s).
- The second group will wrap the clothes and family gifts, labeling them for the recipients in each family.
- The third group will assemble the donated food into baskets and mark them for the appropriate families.

Delivering the Holiday Items to the Families

The delivery of these items is always a meaningful event. Encourage as many staff members as are available to deliver the gifts, trees, and baskets to the families. Sing holiday songs in the car and enjoy a candy cane or other holiday treat to help get into the spirit. With the approval of the family members, take their pictures to post on the bulletin board for all the staff members to see.

 SECRET SANTA DAYS

Participating staff members will write their names on a piece of paper and put them in a hat. Each person then draws a name to determine whose Secret Santa he or she will be. On the designated days, participants secretly deliver their gifts to the person whose name they drew.

Designate the type of gifts to be given on each day and set a price limit on the gifts. Staff members sometimes get carried away when shopping, which can make the group uncomfortable. Setting limits makes the exchanges equitable.

Here is a verse you can use to get the staff excited to participate. *(Debra Macklin, Quincy, MI)*

The Four Days of Secret Santa

When we were little, they spoiled the fun
We believed in Santa, and then they told us there was none.
But little surprises are such wonderful mood-lifters
We've decided to become our own little "gifters."

DAY ONE should find you giving a **SPECIAL HOLIDAY TREAT**
It may be cookies or candies, or even dried meat.
Something that smells and tastes like the season
Or munchies to be enjoyed for any old reason.

DAY TWO will be your chance to **DECORATE THE TREE**
With an ornament that you bought or maybe got for free.
Perhaps you can sew, sculpt, paint, or crochet
Then make it more personal and do not delay.

DAY THREE is your chance to do something very kind
Bring a small item today that will help ease a worried mind.
A little gift that is designed to **RELIEVE THE HOLIDAY STRESS**
Something kind and thoughtful to take minds off of the craziness.

DAY FOUR you'll not only give, but you'll get
And this day will be the best day yet.
Choose a **TOY THAT REMINDS YOU OF THE PERSON YOU DREW**
And the toy will be given to someone needier than you.

Some child, somewhere will know what to do
When they receive the toy that reminds others of you.
And you will know when the holiday is done
That you helped to make someone's holiday more fun.

Possible ideas for designated days include:

Lunch Day

Bring in a fun lunch for the person whose name you drew, including his or her favorite treats. Decorate the bag with holiday designs to give it a festive feel. Not much of a cook? A gift certificate to a fast food restaurant or the school cafeteria, an energy bar, or a peanut butter and jelly sandwich may be just the answer.

Toy Day

Give a toy that represents that person's interest. (e.g., give a toy football to a football fan). The toys can then be donated to organizations such as Toys for Tots or to the families the school is sponsoring.

Cookie Day

Let your creativity run wild! You could bake cookies and deliver them, give animal crackers or other boxed cookies, or perhaps provide a collection of cookie recipes or even a jar of cookie dough to be baked later.

Cookie Mix in a Jar

1 cup	all-purpose flour
1 tsp	ground cinnamon
1/2 tsp	ground nutmeg
1 tsp	baking soda
1/2 tsp	salt
3/4 cup	raisins
2 cups	rolled oats
3/4 cup	packed brown sugar
1/2 cup	white sugar

Mix together flour, ground cinnamon, ground nutmeg, baking soda, and salt. Set aside.

Layer ingredients in the following order into a 1-quart wide mouth canning jar: flour mixture, raisins, rolled oats, brown sugar, and white sugar. It will be a tight fit. Make sure you firmly pack down each layer before adding the next layer.

Decorate the jar and attach a tag with these instructions:

Oatmeal Raisin Spice Cookies

1. Preheat oven to 350°F. Line cookie sheets with parchment paper.

2. Empty jar of cookie mix into large mixing bowl. Use your hands to thoroughly mix.

3. Mix in 3/4 cup butter or margarine, softened. Stir in 1 slightly beaten egg and 1 teaspoon of vanilla. Mix until completely blended. You will need to finish mixing with your hands. Shape into balls the size of walnuts. Place on a parchment-lined cookie sheet, 2 inches apart.

4. Bake for 11 to 13 minutes in preheated oven or until edges are lightly browned. Cool 5 minutes on cookie sheet. Transfer cookies to wire racks to finish cooling.

Stress Reliever Day

Give bubble bath, squish balls, a CD of relaxing music, a meditation book, antacids, chocolate, aromatherapy item, popcorn, etc.

Holiday Break Day

Give items that can be used during the holiday break, such as a book, a crossword puzzle magazine, a pair of movie tickets, TV Guide, etc.

Cartoon Day

Give a funny keychain, cartoon or comic book, calendar, cartoon character figure, etc., to your special person. Wrap it with the Sunday comics from your newspaper.

Next Year Day

Give gifts that could either help or delight your person in the upcoming year. The gift could be a calendar, coffee mug, fitness magazine or book, T-shirt, New Year's Eve party favor, pen, or a "gift of time" such as covering recess or bus duty, etc.

Naughty or Nice Day

Let your imagination run wild! But make sure the naughty is still in good taste.

Homemade Gift Day

You can give food, household items such as a hot pad, a candle, a plant you grew, a CD of your music . . . anything that you made yourself.

Decoration Day

Give a holiday decoration such as a tree ornament, lapel pin, gift wrap, etc.

"It's Beginning to Taste a Lot Like the Holiday"

Share snack foods that are associated with the holidays— candy canes, cookies, fudge, hard candy, cheese and crackers, sausage, fruitcake, etc.

Musical Day

Give a music-related gift such as a musical toy, sheet music for a holiday song, etc.

"It's Beginning to Smell a Lot Like the Holiday"

Give items whose scents remind you of the holiday season— cinnamon sticks, potpourri, candles, cookies, bath oil, mulling spices, peppermint, pine tree fragrance, etc.

GROUP ACTIVITY DAYS

Plan group events according to how much time you will have for them. If they're during lunch, then they will need to be quick and fun. If you do them after the students leave, after school, or during a staff meeting, then they can be more involved. The purpose is to be a stress-relieving, fun get-together. Some activities involve the group as a whole; others require forming smaller groups. Usually, participants in small group events team up with their friends. If you want participants to get to know each other better, consider using the following two activities to form groups.

Holiday Whistle to Form Groups

Write the titles of holiday songs on pieces of paper according to the number of people participating (e.g., three or four). Songs you might use are:

Jingle Bells
The Dreidel Song
Deck the Halls
Jingle Bell Rock
I Saw Mommy Kissing Santa Claus
Santa Claus is Coming to Town
Frosty the Snowman
It's Beginning to Look a Lot Like Christmas

Rudolph the Red-Nosed Reindeer
Auld Lang Syne

Give each person a piece of paper with a song title on it. Then have everyone whistle that song while finding others who are whistling the same tune. Can't whistle? Hum the song instead.

When the group members have found each other, have each group try to whistle their song (while not laughing) to the others so they can guess the title of the song.

I'm Only Half Without You

Give each person a name tag with half a name, movie or song title, phrase, etc., written on it (e.g., one tag has "Santa" and the other has "Claus"). Then let the staff members mingle/ search until they find their partner. Examples of names that can be used are:

Rudolph the Red-Nosed Reindeer
Mrs. Claus
Tiny Tim
Ebenezer Scrooge
Frosty the Snowman
The Grinch Who Stole Christmas
Miracle on 34th Street
It's a Wonderful Life
Christmas Carol
Jack Frost
Babes in Toyland
'Twas the Night Before Christmas
Jolly Old St. Nick
Merry Christmas
Happy Hanukkah

This will form pairs; then have the pairs with the same names form small groups.

The following are some ideas for group activities for the whole gang.

Holiday Sing-Along

Provide the lyrics to well-known holiday songs. If possible, find someone who can accompany the group on the piano. If not, download the music to holiday songs and lead the staff in a group sing-along to boost everyone's spirits during this special time of year.

Watch a Holiday Movie

Show a holiday movie such as *Miracle on 34th Street, It's a Wonderful Life, White Christmas, Christmas Vacation, Scrooge,* etc. You may have to show it over a period of a couple of days. And remember the popcorn!

Name That Holiday Tune

Record "snippets" of the beginnings of holiday songs and have staff members guess the names of the songs.

Holiday Word Searches

Make word searches using holiday-related words. Have each team compete to find the words and give a prize to the winning team.

Dress Like Your Favorite Holiday Item

Encourage staff members to dress up like a holiday gift, tree, reindeer, Santa, elf, etc.

Slippers and Cocoa

At the end of the day, host a social event in which staff members can wear their slippers and drink cocoa. For added fun, have a slipper contest, giving prizes for the funniest, prettiest, most original, etc.

Cookie Exchange

Have each participant bake 1–2 dozen cookies. The cookies are displayed and participating staff members select 1–2 dozen assorted cookies to take home.

Although the participants of this activity have typically been female staff members, the men at Arbor Heights Elementary School in Seattle made this a "guys only" event. What started as a lark became a tradition. The male staff members each bake a dozen cookies, decorate the plates, and prepare for a fun-filled exchange.

They established several rules: ready-baked cookies are not allowed, spouses and significant others may not assist, and don't skimp on the ingredients (use butter). The actual exchange includes playing their favorite music and swapping baking tales of trials and challenges. It's best not to bake the cookies the night before the exchange just in case there are more tribulations than successes.

Build a Snowman

Version #1: If you have snow, suggest that the teams build real snowmen outside. You could set a theme for each year such as sports, TV shows, cartoons, occupations, etc. Have each team meet to design its snowman and then bring in the necessary decorations or clothes/accessories.

Version #2: No snow? Have the groups create their own "non-snow" snowmen. Give each group the same materials such as cardboard, three feet of fabric, buttons, pins, toilet paper, construction paper, tape, etc., and see what they can create within a designated time period. Be sure to take pictures and consider giving prizes for the most artistic/funny/unusual creations.

Version #3: Provide marshmallows, candy, pretzels, and other miscellaneous items for each group, and have them design and build their own snowmen. Display their creative designs.

Candy Cane Hunt

Hide candy canes or other treats in a designated area for staff members to find.

Version #1: Hide the candy canes all over the school (in places students don't frequent) and have staff members search for them throughout the day. At the end of the day,

bring everyone together to count their candy canes. The person with the most candy canes receives a "grand prize": a HUGE candy cane.

Version #2: Hide candy canes in a designated inside or outside area. Blow a whistle to start the search. After the allotted amount of time, blow the whistle again to end the search. The person with the most candy canes gets the "grand prize": a HUGE candy cane. *(Tanya Blehm, Saginaw, MI and others)*

Index —

A

M

T

Y

**Corwin
Press**

The Corwin Press logo—a raven striding across an open book—represents the union of courage and learning. Corwin Press is committed to improving education for all learners by publishing books and other professional development resources for those serving the field of PreK–12 education. By providing practical, hands-on materials, Corwin Press continues to carry out the promise of its motto: **"Helping Educators Do Their Work Better."**

NAESP

NATIONAL ASSOCIATION OF ELEMENTARY SCHOOL PRINCIPALS
Serving All Elementary and Middle Level Principals

Serving All Elementary and Middle Level Principals

The 29,500 members of the National Association of Elementary School Principals provide administrative and instructional leadership for public and private elementary and middle schools throughout the United States, Canada, and overseas. Founded in 1921, NAESP is today a vigorously independent professional association with its own headquarters building in Alexandria, Virginia, just across the Potomac River from the nation's capital. From this special vantage point, NAESP conveys the unique perspective of the elementary and middle school principal to the highest policy councils of our national government. Through national and regional meetings, award-winning publications, and joint efforts with its 50 state affiliates, NAESP is a strong advocate both for its members and for the 33 million American children enrolled in preschool, kindergarten, and grades 1 through 8.